# Building on the Work of Our Elders and Ancestors: Merging STEM with Kawaida to Elevate Blackness (...and everything else...)

On the cover / left-to-right:

Malcolm X, Imhotep, Anna Julia Cooper,
Maulana Karenga (in frame), Mary
McCleod Bethune, Goddess Ma'at,
Franz Fanon

Aminah ShaBazz, Illustrator

## Dedication:

This book is dedicated to my family – those who I know and don't know – and all people who have reconnected with African history and culture in a meaningful way, especially those who inspire others to do the same.

This book is also dedicated to the people and organizations who join us as partners in our work. They are equally committed to our shared goal of promoting daily practice of the Nguzo Saba / Seven Principles to elevate our Blackness – and everything else.

This includes the organizations and people we have worked with – Alkebu-lan Village (Greg McKenzie and Jala Hendrix), the Detroit Black People's Food Sovereignty Network (Malik Yakini and Hanifa Adjuman), and Imagiread Children's Literacy Academy (Tiffany Rashan) all originally from Detroit, MI; PASHI – The Pan African Sisterhood Health Initiative (Maisha Ongoza) and the "All This Math" YouTube Channel (Akil Parker), based out of Philadelphia, PA; Wo'se Community of the Sacred African Way (Bill Johnson) from Oakland, CA; Fourth Power, Inc. (Dr. Asegun Henry) from Cambridge, MA; plus, my wife and children, Sarah, Ameni, and Leymah Baker; and team members Akhir Rashad, Aminah ShaBazz, Arnett Carl Duncan, Kathy Duncan, Ciara Shabazz, and all who support the work done by The Afrikan Restoration Project now or before.

I extend a special dedication to longtime Los Angeles community leader, educator, and student of Kawaida – the Honorable Prof. Amen Rahh – Chair Emeritus, Africana Studies Dept., CSU Long Beach for being a constant source of critical support and encouragement.

Finally, with our efforts so directly linked with the Kwanzaa holiday, this book is dedicated to Kinamo Damu (Terri Bandele) who was the ten-year year-old girl in December 1965 who persistently asked questions that inspired Kwanzaa's creation. We hope to encourage new conversations about Kwanzaa and our children's capacity to inspire and achieve greatness by sharing and honoring her contribution.

In doing this work, we acknowledge the power in asking critical questions and we honor the unlimited capacities of collective work...

# About the author:

Harold Shujaa Baker is a Detroit native, a cultural study group coordinator, a long-time student of Kawaida, and a former member of the African American Cultural Center / Us in Los Angeles where he began learning and teaching about Kwanzaa and the Nguzo Saba / Seven Principles starting in 2005.

He is also an electromechanical designer and prototype engineer with a dynamic, decades long career including design of – space experiments for NASA, energy production and storage systems, medical systems and facilities, plus other commercial and government design projects. He currently provides mechanical design, prototype manufacturing, and short run production services.

For more info see https://vdandp.com.

Shujaa is also cofounder of The Afrikan Restoration Project, a Pan African study group with a fifteen-year long tradition of promoting and providing community based cultural study and organization in southern California. This work continues with annual and periodic events online and in the greater Los Angeles area.

This book project combines all these roles and has been a labor of love to complete...

## About this book:

This book begins as an ethical treatise on how STEM (science, technology, engineering, and manufacturing) should be developed and applied based on lessons found in the social philosophy called Kawaida. Kawaida is a communitarian African philosophy created by Dr. Maulana Karenga that informed creation of the Pan African holiday, Kwanzaa, and the Nguzo Saba / Seven Principles.

The work involved began with a requested review of all existing Kawaida scholarship for the author to extract and develop a Kawaida perspective on STEM. This led to the principles, practices, criticisms, challenges, and goals outlined in this book that reflect a Kawaida perspective on how STEM should be developed and applied. This includes advancing the intent to inspire and create an increasing number of "*sedjemic*" STEM professionals in the global Black community to reclaim our once prominent cultural focus as "*responsible and responsive*" masters of every STEM discipline.

The author, Shujaa Baker, explains how forty years' experience as a STEM professional, twenty years as a student of Kawaida, and more than a decade coordinating cultural study group activities in southern California led to this project. As part of the background discussion, he shares how previously held concerns about possible conflicts between Kawaida philosophy and final teachings from Min. Malcolm X were resolved in conversation with Min. Malcolm's closest associate, the former vice president of his Organization for Afro-American Unity (OAAU), Dr. Earl 5X Grant.

The book concludes with an introduction of an expansive Kawaida STEM project that reflects the lessons in this book and all Seven Principles applied at a high level. This includes introduction of a new multi-function phone app titled "Nguzo Saba 365" and a major update to the https://kwanzaa.org website. This project is based on a variety of new initiatives designed to create an online community and promote daily practice of the Nguzo Saba / Seven Principles as an active strategy to elevate Blackness, and everything else, because the world follows us when we're at our best...

# TABLE OF CONTENTS

## Building on the Work of Our Elders and Ancestors: Merging STEM with Kawaida to Elevate Blackness (...and everything else...)

*"Every generation must, out of relative obscurity, discover its mission and either fulfill it, or betray it." Frantz Fanon, The Wretched of the Earth*

## 1. Introduction

History shows that ideas broad enough to frame new societies are rarely conceived or successfully implemented. New thought systems or philosophies with adequate depth to inform and sustain large communities develop slowly, if at all, just as new ideas to transform existing societies develop slowly, too – and against many odds.

Old and new scholars debate and examine both old and new social philosophies at universities and places of higher learning throughout the world. Some of these new ideas emerge in these relatively safe spaces, while others emerge from revolutionary mass movements – or from a blending of the two – as it happened with a social philosophy called Kawaida.

## A. How This Project Originated

This project began as part of an effort to expand the scope, scale, and reach of Kawaida philosophy. Kawaida is an African centered social philosophy conceived by longtime California State University Africana Studies professor, Dr. Maulana Karenga, during his graduate studies in politics and philosophy in the early 1960's.

Kawaida is a Swahili word that means to practice or uphold "tradition," or to do what is "normal" in a context where shared traditional values, communal harmony, and collective prosperity between people and the environment are the goal.

Dr. Karenga amplifies this by interpreting the word to mean "tradition and reason." Here, Kawaida represents the moral, ethical, and thought basis for a renewed and just society by blending the best of ancient and traditional African wisdom with our most well-reasoned and well-informed modern understanding for the best possible outcomes.

Today, Kawaida is defined to be –

*"A communitarian African philosophy which is an ongoing synthesis of the best of African thought and practice in constant exchange with the world."*

As a leading theorist of the Black Power Movement of the 1960's, Dr. Karenga conceived Kawaida to be a broad-based cultural foundation for a new and improved society structured around the social, political, and economic best interests of Black people and others. In the decades since, he has published a long list of scholarly articles and books that outline and define what Kawaida represents. This includes one of the most widely used textbooks in the field of Africana Studies – Introduction to Black Studies – and original translations of ancient Kemetic / Egyptian sacred texts – The Husia: Sacred Wisdom of Ancient Egypt – among others. For more info, see the University of Sankore Press website or Dr. Karenga's website for available titles and a full publication list.

Many people who have never heard of Kawaida are either familiar with or participants in annual activities that reflect and advance core Kawaida values and principles. That's because Dr. Karenga is most widely known as the creator of the African American and Pan African holiday called, Kwanzaa, which combines with the Nguzo Saba / Seven Principles to represent Kawaida's most widely known offering to the world and its primary point of engagement with the global African community.

A continuing interest in Kwanzaa and the Nguzo Saba remains. Yet, efforts to promote or apply Kawaida as a broad scale social philosophy have been limited since the end of the Black Power Movement in the 1970's.

Kawaida is based primarily on moral and ethical teachings from some of the greatest African societies of antiquity – ancient Kemet, Yorubaland,

8

Dogon, and others – along with other meaningful ideas and practices of modern African and Pan African culture. While other scholars have added to Kawaida scholarship, it primarily reflects Dr. Karenga's work and perspectives as an activist scholar, researcher, and professor of African history and ethics. Past and contemporary scholars and cultural icons are widely quoted and continuously recognized for their contributions through Dr. Karenga's research. For Kawaida to reach its full potential, other current and future scholars must build on its moral and ethical foundation to add perspective and expert insight from every field and discipline necessary to sustain a society.

During the summer of 2019, I was invited to participate in a project with that exact goal.

## B.   The Kawaida Work Group Project

I became a serious student of Kawaida in early 2005 after meeting and talking with Dr. Karenga for the first time after a Kwanzaa event in December 2003. Since then, I have come to believe Kawaida's three greatest strengths are in its grounding in universal African wisdom, its call for continuous development through critical internal and external examination (courageous questioning), and its potential for unlimited forward development through continuing contributions of committed scholars.

During the summer of 2019, I was invited to participate in a new book project where several longtime students and advocates of Kawaida were being asked to write and share a Kawaida perspective on social issues related to their profession or expertise.

As a social philosophy with a moral / ethical foundation, Kawaida's lessons align most readily with various fields of social work, spiritual or religion-based work, and other professions that engage directly with the overall human condition. The disciplines seeming to be the least related to Kawaida's lessons are those grounded in science, technology, engineering, applied mathematics, and manufacturing (STEM&M [TM]).

However, Kawaida does offer teachings that are both relatable and specific to these disciplines, beginning with its earliest texts up to current writings. Since Kawaida ethics are universally relevant, they can be used to inform criteria, interpret values, and define acceptable practices and prohibitions for how we should develop and apply STEM going forward.

Through his writings and teachings on our responsibilities to ourselves, history and humanity, the Creator, and the natural world, Dr. Karenga offers Kawaida insights we can interpret to inspire our broader embrace of STEM while helping to inform a new scientific and technological ethos, thereby *"expand*[ing] *the areas of our productive capacity."* [1 – p.111]

With almost fifteen years of actively studying Kawaida at that time, and over thirty years' experience as a design engineer, multimedia developer, and all-around tech nerd, I was up for the task. I perceived the project as an extension of the computer and technical services I provided for many years as a member, then supporter, of the African American Cultural Center / Us in Los Angeles, including providing a major update to The Official Kwanzaa Website completed in 2018.

I received the invitation to participate in the book project as something of a reward for my committed efforts over the years. As the intended scope of the Kawaida Work Group Project became clear, I was honored and humbled to learn it would be considered the first Kawaida text on technology. So, I got to work!

Oddly enough, it was fortunate this all occurred during COVID19. With its dramatic impact on the Black community and our response to it, and the world on extended COVID lockdown, I had a very relevant critical perspective to write from and an opportunity to read and write full time that would not happen otherwise.

My work began with a careful re-examination of all Kawaida writings, with Dr. Karenga's input to ensure nothing was missed. I then got busy extracting every lesson related to science, technology, engineering, applied mathematics, and manufacturing (STEM&M ™) that I could derive.

Since applied mathematics is built into these disciplines, and manufacturing is not always adequately considered, I interpret STEM throughout this work to mean "science, technology, engineering, and manufacturing."

Our agreement was that I would review all the texts to extract all relevant lessons, then I would add whatever I thought was relevant to create a meaningful context for sharing a Kawaida perspective on STEM. I then wrote a sixty-page paper in two equal parts, where the first part shared a Kawaida perspective on applied STEM as requested.

Everything I wrote in part two related to my own perspectives and my preparation for the project.

There, I explained how I was introduced to Kawaida philosophy and how I resolved potential conflicts I perceived between certain aspects of Kawaida and teachings from Min. Malcolm X in conversation with an 87-year-old elder once known as Brother Earl 5X. Professor Earl Grant, as he came to be most widely known, was the vice-president of Min. Malcolm's Organization for Afro-American Unity (OAAU) and his closest associate during his final years with the NOI and afterward. It was a great honor to get to know him and to have those talks with him.

As an added cultural credential, I shared my experience coordinating a well-attended community-based study group for over a decade in southern California known as The Afrikan Restoration Project. My friend and brother – now an ancestor – Kwesi Osafo and I renamed and coordinated this group after we inherited The Long Beach Study Group in 2009. At that point, the group had met for a culturally based study session almost every Thursday evening for twenty years straight going back to when it was founded after the Association for the Study of Classical African Civilizations (ASCAC) held its annual conference in Kemet / Egypt in 1989.

Also, since my professional expertise is based on a long and active career instead of acquired degrees, I shared some of my technical background, including experience working with the first Black astronaut, Dr. Guion Bluford, while I helped design space flight experiments for NASA.

The background discussion also includes a presentation of how my brother, Akhir Rashad, and I began to merge Kawaida and modern technology with The Official Kwanzaa Website update we completed in 2018, and the supplemental Kwanzaa website we set up separately back then at https://kwanzaa.net. This includes a series of custom Nguzo Saba / Seven Principles themed products we design and manufacture ourselves using 3D modeling software and 3D printing and rapid manufacturing technology.

This section also includes my assessment of what the future holds for Kawaida, ending with my highest aspirations for how Kawaida could be merged with STEM in an applied way going forward.

Out of all that was shared in the paper, I was most excited about presenting a fully developed technology-based proposal to finance and build a modern, multi-level, multi-function facility to serve as "The International Kwanzaa Headquarters" – a project initially conceived a few decades before.

Several participants submitted drafts for the Kawaida Work Group Project in 2020 as the project outline called for. The latest update indicates the project may resume at some point as other projects are completed and more time becomes available for the participants.

In the meantime, and to support our continuing and increasing efforts to merge Kawaida with modern technology for maximum benefit, I have chosen to publish a revised and reformatted version of the draft I submitted as chapters two and three of this work, respectively.

What follows is an updated and revised version of the paper originally titled – "Kawaida Imperatives for Current and Emerging Science and Technology Demands: Improving Our Standing and Focus with Applied Science, Technology, Engineering, and Manufacturing (STEM)."

## C. Objectives for "Building on the Work of Our Elders and Ancestors"

Consistent with the Nguzo Saba / the Seven Principles, we are inspired by seven objectives in this work. These objectives will be met through an interpretation of Kawaida teachings, a discussion of the current engagement between Kawaida and modern technology, a critical assessment of the varied challenges to modern technology being used most effectively for these purposes, and applied suggestions to achieve the goals outlined.

Our primary objective is to continue learning, sharing, and building on the work of our respected elders and ancestors in the most meaningful way. This is an effort to share their teachings and to build upon them, adding the distinct contribution and perspective each of us is capable of if we commit to doing our best work.

The second goal is to interpret Kawaida philosophy to extract vital principles, practices, and prohibitions for all fields of STEM development going forward to serve as an alternative to the profit driven practices quickly driving Earth and people to ruin.

Our third intent is to engage the most effective ways to use applied science and modern technology to advance Kawaida STEM as the basis for a much-needed new ethos to govern how we apply and interact with STEM.

The fourth objective encompasses the second and third as we examine how Kawaida can be more broadly advanced and applied to further inspire our people to reconnect with an even deeper understanding of who we are so we can fully realize ourselves concerning STEM and beyond. When we *"rescue and reconstruct ourselves"* in this way, we will continue in our best tradition, again becoming *"a model and mirror for the world to emulate."* [16]

Fifth, in the applied spirit of the goals of The Kawaida Work Group Project, I look forward to its completion and hope to inspire other committed scholars and Kawaida advocates to do as I have done and write a Kawaida perspective on the social issues and challenges related to their profession or expertise.

By doing so, we can build on the work Dr. Karenga began as a continuation of the work started by countless other African and Pan African scholars before and with him to remind us of our best teachings. That will help us

13

to be more keenly aware of our responsibilities to ourselves and each other today, to then be more highly inspired to meet or exceed those obligations going forward.

In this way, we move closer to fulfilling the original objective for Kawaida to serve as the ethical and organizational foundation for a renewed and just society. To help us get there, we need a Kawaida perspective on every key aspect of society to include a legal, financial, and business analysis, along with a medical or biological analysis, and more specialized technology analyses, among others.

Our sixth objective is to create and use an effective merger of Kawaida and modern technology to promote increased understanding and embrace of the Nguzo Saba / Seven Principles as a daily vocation among Black people. To help make that possible we are introducing a new app called "Nguzo Saba 365" which will provide a way to engage daily with others about how the Seven Principles are being applied around the world.

Our seventh and final goal is to introduce the expansive new Nguzo Saba / Seven Principles themed online community we have created where individuals and organizations can gain and share knowledge and information with other people and organizations who embrace the Nguzo Saba / Seven Principles. We have active partnerships with a core group of organizations and people from around the country who have long term experience with the Nguzo Saba to build upon. As members of our online community, their selected content will be shared through our app and accessible to the millions who visit our website during Kwanzaa season and year-round.

We have expanded our https://kwanzaa.org website to include a new and growing "Kwanzaa For Kids" program where we have children's lessons, activities, and games to help teach children about Kwanzaa and the Nguzo Saba / Seven Principles with reading and technology based lessons. This online space will be used and made available for an unlimited range of STEM and culture-based content and learning activities.

Ultimately, our intent is to begin doing the work Kawaida STEM declares needs to be done by learning and developing technology and using our traditional values to define how we use it. By doing this, we contribute to our generation discovering its mission and making a meaningful contribution towards fulfilling it.

Our goals will be met and our objectives satisfied when our elders and ancestors are pleased and our desired outcomes for ourselves and the world are achieved.

I commit to this work because I believe Kawaida is one of the most thoughtful responses yet to the issues we have struggled against in this society for centuries. More importantly, I believe Kawaida's focus on applied values offers a way to move past all of that, finally, by giving us a new way to understand ourselves and each other based on how we live in the world, as an alternative to race-based thinking that informs and precedes the race-ism and race-ist oppression we struggle against.

In other words, and in the final analysis, I believe our values and committed works have more influence on who we are in this world than our race or skin color. By building on the work of our elders and ancestors in this way, we hope to move at least one step closer to fulfilling the Kawaida mission –

*"To know our past and honor it; to engage our present and improve it; and to imagine a whole new future to be forged in the most ethical, effective, and expansive ways."*

… and there is no more urgent time than now to do it…


## 2. Black People, Kawaida, STEM, and How They Relate to the World We Want to Live In

### A. How a Diminished Standing in STEM Relates to Kawaida, COVID19 and the Urgency of Now

The COVID19 lockdown became an eerily relevant setting to consider Black people's role and standing around the world today in the applied disciplines of STEM. The disproportionately negative impact COVID had on the Black community proves the need for a renewed focus on increasing our knowledge and improving our standing and representation in STEM professions worldwide.

If that wasn't clear prior to COVID19, our lack of an effective collective response to it should make it clear. COVID left us exposed like nothing else has in some time. Our general lack of access to the specialized knowledge and functions needed for an effective, independent understanding of – and response to – the science and technology-based considerations of it was there for all to see.

According to published numbers, Black people lost more friends and loved ones than any other people to what many, perhaps, rightfully call a "plandemic." [17] In this case, the real pandemic is the absence of righteous ethics and principles for how science and technology is applied within the culture – allowing repeated episodes of new pandemics being discovered – or created – for profit and control, or just to see what happens.

We have found ourselves in similar space before. Yet, as before, we have typically been left to choose which outside opinion to trust and believe over others based largely on which one feels right to us. Otherwise, we're doing our best to guess what's going on because we know the official story can't be trusted.

But when we ran low on food, or toilet paper, or other supplies – or imagined doing so as the initial panic set in – we stood in long lines and looked hopefully toward corporations and others outside of our community to continue supplying our needs. Aside from any consideration of a pandemic, this dependency is one of the most active and emerging threats we face – unknowingly, perhaps.

Dr. Karenga addressed this predicament in a book he wrote over four decades ago (1980) where he discussed the need to improve our standing in the varied fields of science and technology, effectively forecasting this moment where we face *"limited possibilities"* for failing to meet our obligations as advised.

In his early text titled Kawaida Theory: An Introductory Outline, Karenga outlines a vision for the future in a chapter titled Kawaida on Ethos, where he explains the need to increase our presence and standing in all functional areas — not just athletics and entertainment — to broadly advance our interests, saying —

*"It is clearly important for us to expand the areas of our productive capacity. We need not condemn athletes and entertainers; only struggle against the cultural tendency to overconcentrate in those areas. After all, a people whose sole or greatest contribution to society is entertainment will never rule itself or society, or even have a meaningful role in its design and direction. To build a nation and contribute to societal and world development, a people must function in as many diverse capacities as society offers for positive self-assertion."* [1 – p.111-112]

As he continues, Karenga's words from over forty years ago anticipate our tentative position and response to the STEM concerns of COVID19 today. He also predicts the inordinate impact godfather figures like Bill Gates, Anthony Fauci, and others have on the world today, along with godfather companies like Microsoft, Apple, and the pharmaceutical industry, saying —

*"We are obviously deficient in representation and focus in science, technology, and math sciences — yet this is the wave of the future. Technocrats and scientists will no doubt have an even more prominent role in the near future in the design and direction of society. Thus, if we shun these areas and limit ourselves to song, dance, and gladiator sports, we not only reinforce racist images and structures, but limit our future possibilities."* [1 – p.112]

For every deficiency we have in *"science, technology, and math sciences,"* we have equal or greater deficiencies in manufacturing. Simply put, we don't make enough of the products we need in our daily lives, particularly here in America — even basic needs. Our continuing dependency on corporations and those outside of our community to meet these needs is an equal or greater threat to our sovereignty and long-term survival than the predicted *"surprise outbreak"* [17] of COVID19 was and continues to be.

Consistent with this paper's call for Black people to urgently increase our numbers in STEM fields across the board today, tomorrow, and going forward, Dr. Karenga also lamented our related *"lack of* [a collective or] *national vocation"* saying –

> *"Kawaida contends that to be alive and active, a nation must have a collective vocation, a self-conscious sense and choice of mission which reflects a positive and expansive identity, purpose, and direction. This vocation will be of necessity rooted in and reflective of that nation's values and views of self, society, and the world and the possibilities inherent in each. It is clear that it is not enough for us to simply be what nature has made us. We must dare to discover and reach the limits of our possibilities. For as argued [elsewhere], we can only create and know ourselves thru such daring and achievement."* [1 – p.103)

Our limited engagement with STEM, and our even more limited recognition as STEM innovators and manufacturers of products we need today leaves us exposed, and departs, confusingly, from our ancestor's now worldwide recognition as the originators of the principal disciplines of STEM. Our ancestors were also the first to apply knowledge of STEM in brilliant and revolutionary ways to build and manufacture whatever they needed, including the grandest monuments and structures from the ancient world requiring STEM knowledge that is either not yet fully understood, or not appropriately credited.

I mean, how were the Great Pyramids built, anyway, and what was their true original purpose? [19]

Our ancestor's advanced knowledge of STEM assisted them in organizing the first advanced societies in human history, making our more recent departure from STEM even more curious, though not completely inexplicable. Despite repeated and brilliant resistance, we have not yet fully recovered from the brutal inhumanities imposed upon us. Like our ancestors, we bear responsibility for responding effectively to it all, since no one will save or restore us but us.

By observing our lack of a collective vocation, Dr. Karenga shares awareness of a core self-conceptual deficit that can be addressed with Kawaida teachings on STEM. By merging modern technology with *"the best of African thought and practice"* in various ways, we develop meaningful tools to inspire a greater understanding of – and reconnection with – our broader history and our foundation as ancient STEM innovators reborn.

Surely, we need to emerge from the perspective where we exist principally as observers or victims of modern science unfolding, or as mere consumers or targets of modern technology to reemerge in completeness, as the best possible versions of ourselves. To do this, we must broadly reinterpret and elevate our self-understanding in every way – including as principled creators, innovators, and users of STEM.

So, in addition to increasing our numbers in STEM, *"Our task,"* – as Dr. Karenga describes it – *"is to synthesize the growth of science and technology with the need for human sensitivity and morality."* [1 – p.113] Simply put, that requires inspiring the greatest number of people possible to become the best possible version of themselves in STEM fields and beyond by developing into what Karenga describes as a *"sedjemic"* person. [6 – p.246]

In his book, Maat: The Moral Ideal in Ancient Egypt, Dr. Karenga outlines the type of applied STEM professional needed for these purposes by describing a person who is accomplished in their discipline, and wisely *"responsive and responsible"* [6 – p.253] to their environment and world circumstance. In the absence of this type of moral grounding, we face the prospect of creating more people motivated by the same values and pursuits of the dominant culture that bring us to the current crisis moment.

Karenga implores Black people to remember who we are and to remain aligned with the distinct moral and natural considerations that distinguish us in our African worldview from the reckless ways and means of the dominant culture. He addresses how the dominant culture's claims toward dominating nature are increasingly being revealed as the fallacy they are -- with climate change raging. He then reminds us, again, of our related responsibility in this moment, writing –

*"Finally, in this focus on science and technology, we must never lose the humanistic and natural emphasis of our cultural concept of soul. Our oppressor has sold his soul for money and machines and in his drive to conquer and control nature has lost his humanity and naturalness. He saw humanization as simple conquest and control rather than creating a context for a higher level of human life. Thus, even though he conquered nature, it has become again his enemy as pollution, ecological imbalance, etc. And instead of emancipating the human personality, he has used science and technology to increase the ways and means of domination.*

*Our task is to synthesize the growth of science and technology with the need for human sensitivity and morality. In this way, we contribute to the historical project of humanizing nature without denaturalizing and dehumanizing humans."* [1 – p.112-113]

This section closes with an admonishment to *"African and other Third World peoples to demonstrate and realize"* [1 – p.113] our full humanity by developing and using our talents to their fullest potential, both individually and collectively. This is important because the distinctions between our values and the dominant society's values require us to place ourselves in decision making positions at every level if we are to help undo the harm – and prevent further harm – to people and the environment caused by profiteers leading the world to ruin. By necessity, this includes improving our representation, related mastery, and moral focus in STEM fields because of the significance of these disciplines in the world.

Surely, if we want to improve our present and future collective response to COVID19 and other manmade or natural threats, we absolutely must increase the number of culturally grounded professionals in every field of applied STEM. But not only that, we must do so with a renewed embrace and understanding of our highest moral and ethical values and practices. Otherwise, we are at risk of duplicating the ways and errors of those temporarily shielded from the global suffering they create.

## B. Reading Kawaida Ethos for STEM from Ancient Texts and Modern Insights

Many of Kawaida's lessons on the rightful way to engage STEM are found in Dr. Karenga's many writings on the environment, from his oldest publications to the most recent.

Over thirty years ago (1990), in another original translation and reinterpretation of sacred African text titled The Book of Coming Forth by Day: The Ethics of the Declarations of Innocence, he lays the basis for Kawaida concerns with destruction and depletion of the environment, and the general human failure to protect and preserve the world for our survival and future generations.

In the Ethical Commentary section of Chapter 3 titled Obligations to Nature, Karenga begins a critique of the then emerging, now imminent, climate crisis where he poses a new environmental ethos as the solution to frame a rightful relationship with the environment, explaining –

*"The world, as a common ecological environment, is currently under several kinds of pressure, including the problems of pollution of air, water and soil, and depletion of other natural resources. The threats to the environment not only affect the possibilities of future generations, but the very existence of the world as we know it. Clearly, an ethics that links life in a holistic framework and makes it morally compelling to respect both the social and the natural is needed."* [3 – p.101]

Here, the text offers language that compels a complete departure from modern modes and methods where man and material are exploited in mass for the profit-based benefits of a few. Staying the course, at this point, it seems, reflects a knowing or unknowing willingness to participate in the untimely and accelerated pillaging and depletion of Earth to benefit the ruling minority.

The discussion continues with a reference to Kawaida's environmental position being based in ancient Kemetic ethical thought – Maat – and the *"indestructible"* link it establishes between people, the Creator, and the natural world with all its occupants. Karenga teaches that –

*"Maatian ethics stresses... a holistic approach, positing an indestructible unity of the human, Divine, and natural. It is, even in its ancient form, committed to a just, good and righteous order in the social and natural realm. From this, one can evolve a social and environmental ethics which are interrelated and interdependent. In fact, the obligation to preserve the environment for ourselves and future generations derives from the same ethics to preserve and promote human life and development. For it compels us not to do anything which would deny or diminish the chances for a full and fulfilling life for each and every person."* [3 – p.101-102]

Continuing, the text harshly criticizes the ultimately self-destructive nature of the predatory capitalist world as a violation of ancient African ethics with practices that fundamentally defy our understanding of what it means to be human. The profit-driven madness further defies our obligations to ourselves, other people, the world and its other occupants, and the Creator who blessed us with these things. The text reads –

*"It is, thus, unethical, in a Maatian sense, to destroy or damage nature, for it eliminates or diminishes chances for a full and fulfilling human life. Moreover, it violates a trust posed in Kheti's concept of responsible trusteeship. Therefore, when we pollute the seas with waste and oil spillage, destroy wilderness areas and rain forests for profit, poison air and water, we violate a divine and human trust. It violates also the obligation posed in the Declarations of Innocence not to be arrogant and assume the earth exists simply for our utility for the moment with no thought of what it means to animal and plant life or future generations. This is anthropocentrism at its worse, a self-centeredness that is not only detrimental to nature, but in the end, also to the reckless, destructive and uncaring person which it creates."* [3 – p.102]

The next passage speaks poetically of our obligations as caretakers of the world and the threats to our own existence and quality of life, and that of future generations when we fail to meet those obligations. Here, Karenga specifically calls out the industrial and energy sectors whose profit pursuits led to environmental destruction and nuclear waste and devastation like Three Mile Island in the U.S., Chernobyl in Russia, and more recently, Fukushima in Japan.

Dr. Karenga also specifically criticizes the bio-technology and bio-warfare industries with its foundations in smallpox blankets, the Tuskegee Experiment, then on to HIV/AIDS, COVID19, and other morally monstrous diseases writing –

> "[Our] *ethic of care and responsibility toward nature requires us to preserve nature for future generations. Our posterity has a right to see whales and elephants alive rather than in films and photos, to drink clean water and breathe unpolluted air and enjoy beaches unmarred by waste. And to pollute and poison the earth, air and water, to deplete nonrenewable resources of the planet is to erode the quality of human life for the future and thus violate the rights of future generations. Likewise, the nuclear and industrial technology [and bio-technology] which threaten the earth also threaten future generations as well as those living now. Here the virtue of justice is required also for nature, ourselves and others, including future generations."* [3 – p.103]

Kawaida undeniably reflects a broad, new ethos here – based on ancient ideals, of course – that departs fully from prevailing capitalist values. It is a complete roadmap for our obligation to give primary regard to the environment and broad human interests in all of our efforts over the *"gross materialism of the dominant culture"* [16] and society at large.

By following these principles, we can fully enjoy life during our stay on Earth, while creating and leaving the same opportunity for future generations to enjoy more abundantly. For, in this way, as the teachings say, we live for eternity.

*"The very existence of future generations depends on the ethical character and behavior of persons alive now. It is, thus, morally compelling that we strive to limit damage to the earth, curtail and end wasteful consumerism, and respect the claims of nature – animate and inanimate – on us. As the ancient Egyptians taught, if we wish to live for eternity, we must build for eternity. And as Seba Kheti taught, 'Every day is a donation to eternity and even one hour is a contribution to the future.'"* [3 – p.103-104]

Dr. Karenga continues building on Kawaida doctrine related to STEM in his most recent writings, offering clear ethical guidance for the proper way to engage and use natural spaces and resources.

In his article titled, Earth, Wind, Water and Fire: Saving Ourselves and the World, to commemorate World Water Day and Earth Day, respectively, Karenga invokes more traditional African insights from ancient Kemet, encouraging us –

*"...to engage in focused reflection and action directed toward addressing this world-encompassing dual challenge of environmental crisis and environmental care."* [13]

Here, he calls on all people to give –

*"...serious and sustained consideration and active empathetic concern to... providing what is necessary for the health and well-being of the earth and all its inhabitants, especially its most vulnerable."* [13]

This leads to a detailed reflection on the ancient Kemetic concept of *"serudj ta,"* where Karenga writes –

*"The second set of ancient Egyptian Maatian texts [found in The Husia: Sacred Wisdom of Ancient Egypt] teaches us the ethical imperative of*

24

*serudj ta – to constantly repair, renew and remake the world, making it more beneficial and beautiful than we inherited it. For the sacred texts teach that the world is constantly damaged by what we do wrong and fail to do right and thus, we must constantly be concerned with maintaining and restoring the well-being of the world."* [13]

The text elaborates further on this concept of *"serudj ta,"* explaining that –

*"In the fullness of the practice of serudj ta, we are 'to raise up that which is in ruins; to repair that which is damaged; to rejoin that which is severed; to replenish that which is depleted; to strengthen that which is weakened; to set right what is wrong; and to make flourish that which is fragile, insecure and undeveloped.'"* [13]

These lessons, he explains are –

*"...not only for those living, but also to honor those who taught us world-preserving ways to live, work and relate in the world; and for those who come and continue after us..."* [13]

Also, to affirm the interrelated nature of all things in a Kawaida context, and our ultimate obligations to ourselves and all that is in our midst, Karenga writes –

*"Thus, if we are to do good and give the best of ourselves to save the earth and all in it - animate and inanimate - we must clearly and strongly understand and engage it as a simultaneous saving of ourselves. For it is not only the life of the earth that is at stake, but also our own lives."* [13]

This text collectively highlights the inward and outward focus of traditional African social values, their concern with individual development toward the greater good for the community as a whole, and their preoccupation with caring for the world around us. Therefore, there is much we can learn from these –

*"...ancient African ethical texts which speak to the centrality of the natural world in our lives, its provision of life-giving and life-sustaining good, and our implicit and explicit moral obligation to constantly repair, renew and remake the world, making it more beautiful and beneficial than we inherited it..."* [13]

These teachings are a clear departure from the gross individual – and isolated group – thinking that prevails over the dominant culture and the world order today. The related confusion makes it critically important and necessary for African people worldwide to be reminded of these teachings so we can fully embrace the related obligations as a way to inspire the same in others. We must lead by example, *"Because,"* as it is often said in Kawaida – *"...if we won't do it, who will?"* [16]

In this same article, we are reminded of the cultural continuity and broadly shared appreciation for the natural world among traditional African cultures through lessons from the Yoruba ethical and spiritual tradition, Ifá. The Kawaida interpretation deeply respects the spiritual and ritual aspects of Ifá, but focuses principally on the moral narrative and related lessons found in Dr. Karenga's translation of the sacred text titled Odù Ifá: The Ethical Teachings. [5]

Among other things, Ifá ethos is notable for its focus on good character presentation, continuous development throughout our lives, and the willingness for righteous sacrifice in the spirit of community for the good we seek to create. He writes –

*"The sacred text Odù Ifá (33.2) tells us we must "take responsibility for the world, bear the responsibility well and do good for the world." Moreover, the sacred text teaches us that in carrying out this important life-sustaining task, we must stop sacrificing in pursuit of wealth, luxury,*

*comfort and pleasures that threaten and degrade the earth and instead practice a sacrifice that protects and sustains it.* "[13]

Here, Ifá projects those who plunder and pollute the world for profit as Earth's enemies, while reminding us, again, that people bear righteous responsibility for the world. In this text, going further, Ifá not only condemns those who plunder the world, but also those who standby without doing anything to stop it. Karenga reminds us –

*"Indeed, Odù Ifá (10:5) says "the people of the world should stop making sacrifices for wealth and instead make sacrifices that will protect the earth from its enemies," i.e., plunder, pollution and depletion on every level. The sacred text also tells us that "In this way we will live," i.e., survive and thrive. Thus, it concludes, "And so, we should ask earnestly and humbly of each other that as long as we live on earth, that the earth not be destroyed," i.e., either by our hand or those of others, by what we do wrong or fail to do right or by not holding ourselves or others ethically and politically accountable."* [13]

In this closing portion of the article, we see evidence of the deeply spiritual nature of these African cultural teachings as interpreted here in the Kawaida tradition. The Yoruba tradition, Ifá, and the ancient Kemetic tradition, Maat, mentioned here generally reflect traditional African cultural reverence toward the environment and nature, most broadly. In fact, the Kemetic word "Ntr," – which the word "nature" is derived from – is a principal word for the Hidden One, or the all-powerful Creator known as God. [16]

Here, we also see evidence of African people's profound respect and appreciation for ancestors, their righteous appreciation for the gift of life and all that is in it, and their righteous intent to show their respect and appreciation for these things through good deeds. Karenga teaches –

*"Therefore, we are to walk gently, act justly and relate rightly in and for the world. And with the honored ancestors, we hope and say, "May we*

*be granted life, prosperity and health, the blessings of being (and enduring) on earth; knowledge of the right and good (Maat) like the One who created it, and a deep and clear understanding of all that is to be done. Hotep. Ase. Heri."* [13]

Through these writings, and others, Dr. Karenga has outlined the Kawaida perspective on STEM development grounded in modern moral and ethical thought informed by, or based upon, the best of ancient African moral and ethical ideals. Inasmuch as Kawaida philosophy is defined to be *"the best of African thought and practice in constant exchange with the world,"* it is in our collective best interests to examine these teachings more extensively as a source for ideas and recommended practices for a new way to relate to the world thru STEM. This way, we realize ourselves in the fullest while being constantly prepared to respond most effectively to future manmade disasters like COVID19, impending environmental collapse, and all emerging STEM related concerns.

## C. Kawaida Principles, Practices, Criticisms, and Challenges for STEM Development

Whereas other scholars provide analyses from varied technical perspectives on ancient and modern STEM development throughout Africa and the Diaspora, Dr. Karenga's work provides ethical and moral teachings and essential principles to help define strategies and set necessary restrictions for how STEM should be applied in the world. Surely, these principles apply to every human endeavor, but particularly to the fields of STEM.

No critical area of human activity is dismissed from consideration. But with the prominent role STEM purveyors, *"technocrats and scientists* [have and] *will no doubt* [continue to] *have in the design and direction of society,"* it is critically important that we give specific attention to the thought systems and values informing STEM related pursuits. After all, most of the world's worst leaders in history either were – or had immediate access to – skilled and qualified STEM professionals.

Our concern with a noble STEM development ethos is of no value unless we also work to increase the number of qualified people committed to putting that noble STEM ethos into practice in every related field and discipline. Surely, we must use modern technology in the most effective way to advance this mission. Therefore, a review of challenges to forwarding Kawaida STEM, specifically, and Kawaida philosophy more generally will be shared in an upcoming section.

As for the current focus, Kawaida teachings on applied STEM development consider the necessary relationship between people, STEM, the environment, and viable economic activity. The following list of essential principles are offered to frame and inform current and future STEM development toward the best and highest possible outcomes.

I.    **Essential Kawaida STEM Principles**

a.    **Kawaida STEM is informed by the past, and is grounded in the work and struggle efforts of today to benefit ourselves and the world going forward into eternity.**

As with Kawaida generally, its strategies for STEM development are grounded in the best of African historical thought, calling for the highest levels of moral wisdom in its application and exchange with the world today. This, so our efforts will endure going forward to protect and improve the condition of the world and related life choices for our people in the future and into eternity.

This effort begins with a reaffirmation of our history as creators and leading innovators of STEM, as well as being the world's first people to successfully apply and implement STEM at high levels to create the world's first advanced societies. Ancient African people's mastery of STEM disciplines is reflected in the many ancient monuments, temples, remaining structures, and books that serve as timeless evidence of what morally and ethically balanced African people have done, and therefore, can do in the process of fully realizing ourselves.

29

b.  **STEM related thought and development are a distinct component of culture.**

Kawaida philosophy teaches us the values that inform the way a society approaches and applies STEM development are distinctly representative of the culture from which it emerges. As Dr. Karenga is known to say –

*"Ideas don't drop in from the sky or sail in from the ocean. They come from the social context in which we find ourselves."* [16]

With that, history clearly shows how different cultures have engaged the pursuit and application of STEM in profoundly different ways. In this way, the values and practices that inform this truth are a direct reflection of the values, practices, and broader objectives of those who control the society. While there is a clear distinction between the way different cultures have pursued and applied STEM development over time, there is no legitimate way to isolate STEM disciplines as a function of distinct racial or cultural identity.

In other words, there is no "White/European Chemistry" or "Black/African Physics," for example. [16] Yet, the record shows clear differences in the way White/European and Black/African societies have separately pursued and applied STEM throughout history, with distinctly different outcomes, generally, but some similarities. No society has a completely unblemished moral record where applied STEM is concerned, but European culture stands alone for its capacity and willingness to commit the most egregious STEM atrocities.

The Kawaida perspective on STEM, then, emerges from *"the best of African thought and practice* [on STEM related matters] *in constant exchange* [and principled development] *with the world"*.

Consistent with African culture generally, I offer and advance this Kawaida interpretation and perspective towards the greatest possible outcomes with reverence and appreciation to the Divine and natural forces responsible for our existence. This, to advance our culture for future generations to enjoy and build upon in their own time.

c. **STEM development must align with principles of African and human excellence at the highest levels with related goals and objectives to serve the greatest human interests.**

African excellence requires that we achieve the highest levels possible in our understanding and application of STEM to be merged in practice with our highest morality and the most mutually beneficial engagement with the world around us and its other inhabitants.

This idea is informed by the ancient Kemetic teaching on "the perfectibility of the human person," [6 – p.230] which posits that human beings can be developed toward ever increasing levels of self-mastery through the accumulation of broad-based knowledge and the application of true moral wisdom. In keeping with this tradition, Kawaida teachings on STEM development call for those involved to reflect the highest possible levels of human excellence in their STEM related pursuits, in particular, along with an unquenchable desire to achieve ever higher levels.

In fact, <u>AFRICA Means Excellence</u> TM is a trademark of the founding organization of Kawaida (Us) as will be shown in an upcoming applied use of modern STEM example.

d. **Kawaida strategies for STEM are consistent with Kawaida teachings more broadly that inform and encourage a constant pursuit of balance between righteous human needs and our responsibilities to ourselves, one another, the world around us, and the Divine forces of nature (Ntr) that make life possible.**

This manifests as primary concern about the environment, economics, politics, and the human condition in general that requires constant active, organized efforts and struggle to protect and advance our best interests, resist all efforts opposed to us, and maintain a harmonious balance.

Given the critical state of decline in our midst, these teachings urgently implore governments, corporations, and the public at large to embrace and uphold *"the* [ancient African] *ethical imperative of serudj ta –* [which calls for us] *to constantly repair, renew and remake the world, making it more beneficial and beautiful than we inherited it."* [13]

This is the only way we can recover from the current plandemic – COVID19 – and the real pandemic, the moral and ethical crisis that provides for and rewards STEM efforts being misused and abused in this way.

There is an indisputable interrelationship between STEM and all issues involving the environment, economics, politics, and the human condition in general -- requiring primary concern for maintaining the proper balance in all STEM development efforts and applications. This is the only way for human beings to live a good life on Earth.

e.  **Relentless criticism of the dominant culture's misuse and abuse of STEM, and proposing righteous alternatives are essential functions in the Kawaida ethos on STEM.**

If we are to use STEM effectively to help restore a harmonious balance in the world, we must not only use it in the most righteous ways ourselves, but we must also be a constant source of righteous criticism of others who misuse STEM in a way that promotes plunder, pollution, exploitation, death, and general imbalance. These criticisms emerge from the African and Kemetic ideal of *"courageous questioning"* as referenced several times in [The Husia: Sacred Wisdom of Ancient Egypt]. [2]

In his article titled Retrieving the African Ideal: A Courageous Questioning in These Times, Karenga refences these teachings, explaining that –

*"...courageous questioning is a righteous calling into question, seeking answers and offering a severe criticism of the evil, the wrong and the unjust. In addition, it is constantly seeking and speaking truth to the people and to power, demanding justice and bringing Maat (truth, justice, propriety, harmony, balance, reciprocity, and righteous order) into being.*

*And it especially means doing this without fear of consequences of death, political imprisonment, exile, underground existence, and constant attacks of all kinds – or without deference to debilitating and oppressive conditions, customs, hierarchies, or perverse and pathetic calls for peace without justice."* [12]

In order to effectively meet the obligations of this principle, we must not only draw from a spirit of *courageous questioning* alone. Our *courageous questioning* must also be appropriately informed. Karenga clarifies this added requirement in the same article, where he shares a *"list of virtues an activist intellectual possesses,"* saying –

*"These virtues are being: versed in the texts, clear of vision, insightful, well-mentored, deliberate, patient, courageous in questioning; and wise in listening to the ancestors."* [12]

In this context, being *"versed in the texts"* means that in order to offer righteous criticism grounded in *"courageous questioning,"* we must also achieve and sustain an adequate mastery of the related disciplines.

With that, this principle implores Kawaida to continuously explore new and innovative ways to engage our people in STEM disciplines and pursuits so we command the required knowledge to not only challenge misuse and abuse of STEM, but to also pose and practice more righteous alternatives.

## II. Essential Kawaida STEM Practices

The essential practices of Kawaida STEM outlines the daily activities we must engage in to advance these ideas and the outcomes they pursue.

a. **Mastery of chosen discipline**

Ancient Kemetic / African concepts of human excellence explains that people are perfected through the accumulation of knowledge and moral wisdom. In this spirit, Kawaida STEM calls for all people to pursue and gain functional knowledge of modern technology, and for those who align with the principles shared here to gain the highest-level mastery possible in their chosen STEM discipline. The ultimate value of these teachings lies in the number of people who embrace them and the level of mastery achieved in every STEM discipline by them in route to achieving the stated goals.

b. **Focused pursuit and application of STEM that broadly serves the best interests of people and the environment**

As a complete departure from the dominant culture and current circumstances, Kawaida STEM calls for us to only pursue STEM development that serves the greatest good for the greatest number of people and the world around us.

This specifically includes avoiding STEM efforts that promote either small- or large-scale profit pursuits as a primary concern where people or the environment suffer. This includes, but is not limited to, all efforts that abuse and exploit natural resources to the point of pollution or depletion, unrighteously displace or oppress local populations, desecrates sacred spaces, as well as any other efforts that places minority group or ruling class interests as the prevailing concern.

By necessity, this must include a STEM needs analysis to identify areas that require focused attention. To make this effort as worthwhile as possible, we must give some consideration to those things that are essential to our survival daily and in crisis settings like the current COVID context. Ideally, that will lead to short- and long-term plans to develop the necessary talent and fill the required voids to ensure that our community no longer relies on people and companies outside of our community to provide our basic needs. With that, seeking to fully restore and increase the numbers of traditional Black farmers is important.

There are many other programs or initiatives to be developed toward this end. A scientific analysis and verification committee is a related consideration. We certainly do need to maintain a pool of qualified STEM professionals to offer guidance for STEM related emergencies and conditions like COVID, so we don't find ourselves, again, facing "limited possibilities" and little more than wishful thinking when crises and daily life happens.

c.  **Ancient technology review, current technology monitoring and analysis, and future technology development**

In a STEM context, it is consistent with the overall Kawaida mission to *"rescue and reconstruct our history and humanity"* [16] to apply our developed STEM knowledge to carefully evaluate or reevaluate certain past or ancient technologies. We would do this to ensure related lessons have been fully learned and revealed with appropriate credit given. There are many examples, but none are potentially more meaningful than addressing the lingering questions about how the Great Pyramids were built and for what purpose.

It is inconceivable that modern STEM scholarship can't provide definitive answers to those questions. However, it is completely conceivable that the answers to those questions would reveal that our Kemetic ancestors had even greater STEM knowledge than the modern world has already begrudgingly recognized.

To appropriately trained eyes, the remains of the Great Pyramids offer clear evidence of the ways and means by which granite stones, thousands of pounds in mass, were precision machined, located, and fitted within tolerances [18] equal to precision processes of today. Ancient remains of varied components within these structures reveal the ancient Kemetu had discovered and successfully harnessed the power of electricity for practical purposes. That evidence aligns with several artistic renderings found carved on the stone walls of temples and tombs depicting light bulbs, connecting wires, and other components being used to illuminate the ancient Kemetic world. [20 – p.5,25,45,107]

With that, imagine the world having to admit that credit previously assigned to Benjamin Franklin, or Thomas Edison, or even Nikola Tesla for being first to constrain electricity for practical purposes belongs to ancient African people. How would that revelation impact society at large? How would that admission impact Black people around the world? Perhaps, more importantly, how should that reality impact Black people today? Would it help to restore our self-understanding as STEM innovators and beyond?

Besides that, varied mechanical and electrical components, and chemical residue remaining inside the Great Pyramid today proves that it never served as a tomb for Kemetic royalty. The evidence shows the Great Pyramid was a power plant capable of generating high levels of electrical energy. An accurate explanation of the remains details a sequence where vibration and sound were being converted to generate the power needed to drive the greatest civilization in antiquity – without burning fossil fuels.

On a related note, the remaining structures also show evidence of catastrophic failure that, when properly interpreted, could add depth and perspective to our understanding of why this once great society collapsed.

I believe the highest aspiration for Kawaida STEM in this regard is to not only adequately examine and confirm the related evidence, but to also create a scaled reproduction of the Giza Power Plant [18] if the reported evidence is, in fact, true. That would be as revolutionary an act toward rescuing and reconstructing the legacy of African STEM as

Kawaida has been for rescuing and reconstructing the African moral and ethical legacy.

The current technology monitoring and analysis function will stay actively informed about and engaged with the most current STEM products, breakthroughs, and trends with a focus on sustainable technologies that align with Kawaida STEM developmental values. In this practice, Kawaida STEM would also function as a community reference and resource for qualified STEM information and guidance

Of course, we should also focus targeted energy and knowledge at conceiving new forms and methods to apply and develop STEM. Both efforts would be perfectly consistent with the scope and scale of what Kawaida STEM should ultimately represent.

d. **Building of programs and institutions to develop and house our STEM aspirations**

Those who embrace Kawaida STEM must seek to build on its foundation in service and struggle to build STEM related programs and institutions. There are many ways online efforts can be created to promote these teachings and for those who support them to actively engage with one another. In fact, an entirely new app and online community with a Kwanzaa for Kids and a Kawaida STEM focus will be introduced here.

More broadly, an online Kawaida Institute has been discussed in the past and is waiting to be realized. There are more than enough highly qualified people who would support this effort if asked. With the right people in place, modern technology can be used to address all funding needs.

Whereas a limited number of large donors or tax dollars have funded such aspirations in the past, today's technology and social media has created crowd funding, where related information is quickly shared with large numbers of people, allowing those interested to respond with large or small donation or investment funds that can quickly add up. Also, viral online content generates resources based on the number of hits. The continuing popularity of Kwanzaa and the Nguzo

Saba / Seven Principles make this a viable approach to secure at least some portion of the needed resources.

This ideal is one of many that calls for a Kawaida economics and business ethos to be similarly outlined, as well as other Kawaida interpretations for other professions and disciplines, like law.

All Kawaida STEM innovations provide unlimited opportunity to engage the sixth principle of the Nguzo Saba – Kuumba / Creativity – particularly, and all other principles, in their conception and creation. The programs and efforts that could exist based on these ideals are only limited by our imagination and willingness to pursue them.

For example, I will share some of my experience with modern STEM by offering a class on 3D printing for children, teens, and adults. I would teach those enrolled how to select, set up, and use a FDM (fused deposition modeling) printer that can cost less than $200 to purchase these days. FDM printers use melted plastic to literally grow products out of plastic by "printing" one very thin layer at a time, as thin as .003" thick.

I would also show how printable models can be located on the internet at no cost or at cost, based on the application. This would allow children to locate 3D models of toys they like on the internet to be downloaded and 3D printed for their enjoyment. Teens and adults could locate their own toys or tools of any sort, or tools to be printed. A follow-up class could teach people how to create their own custom 3D design models.

I have used 3D printers professionally since the early 1990's when I helped design low orbit space experiments at the NASA Glenn Research Center. The team of designers, engineers, physicists, and other scientists I worked with on the SAMPIE Project [21] (from 1991-1994) created the first space experiment developed at the Glenn Research Center using 3D solid modeling software and 3D printing for prototype manufacturing. That experiment flew aboard Space Shuttle Columbia on NASA Mission STS-62 in March 1994.

I worked at <u>NASA Glenn</u> as a consultant on my next project, the <u>Microscale Hydrodynamics Study</u>, [22] and created the first 3D animation ever used for a space experiment developed there. To make that experience even better – as a brief aside – two of my most cherished possessions are letters of commendation I received for my work there from the first Black astronaut, Dr. Guion Bluford [23], who was hired to lead the company I worked for after he retired as an astronaut. I was thankful to have an opportunity for a one-on-one meeting with him while I was there. That was awesome!

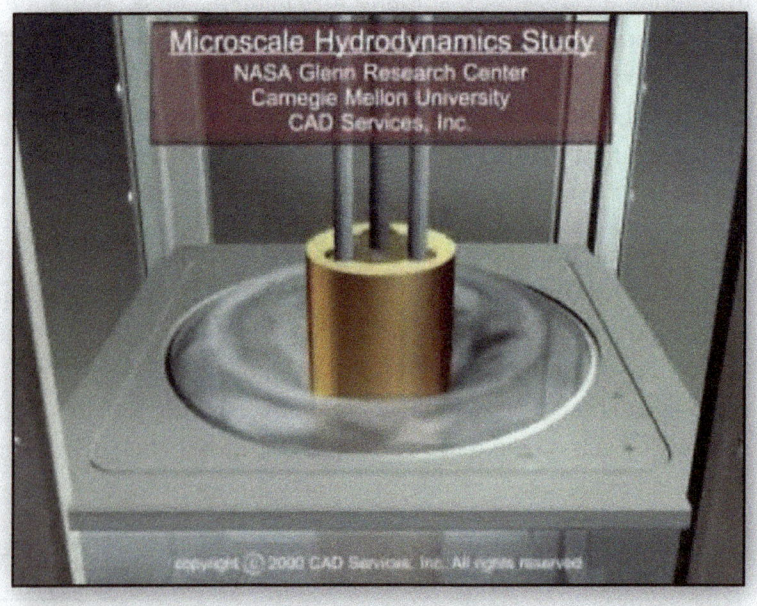

Screen capture of 3D animation I produced to simulate on orbit operation of the Microscale Hydrodynamics Study.

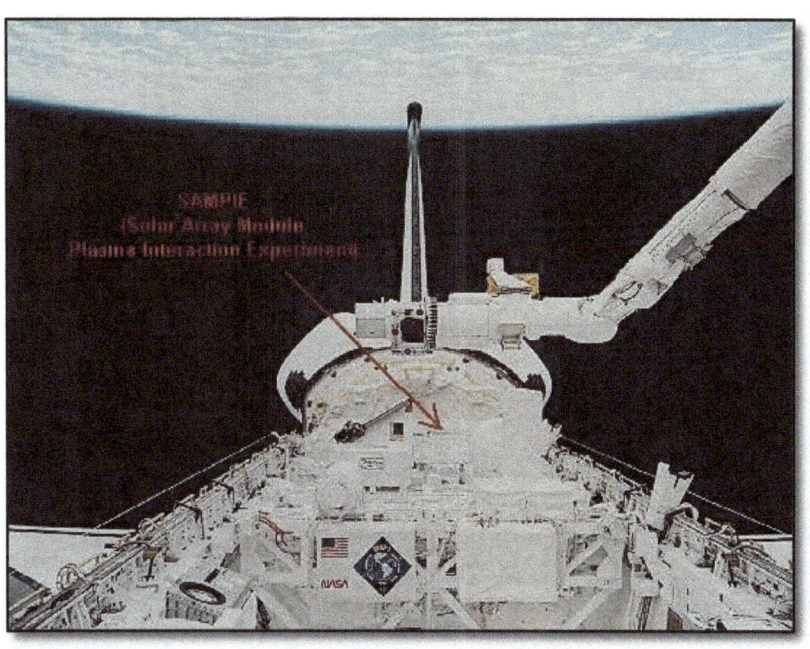

Solar Array Module Plasma Interaction Experiment (SAMPIE) on orbit

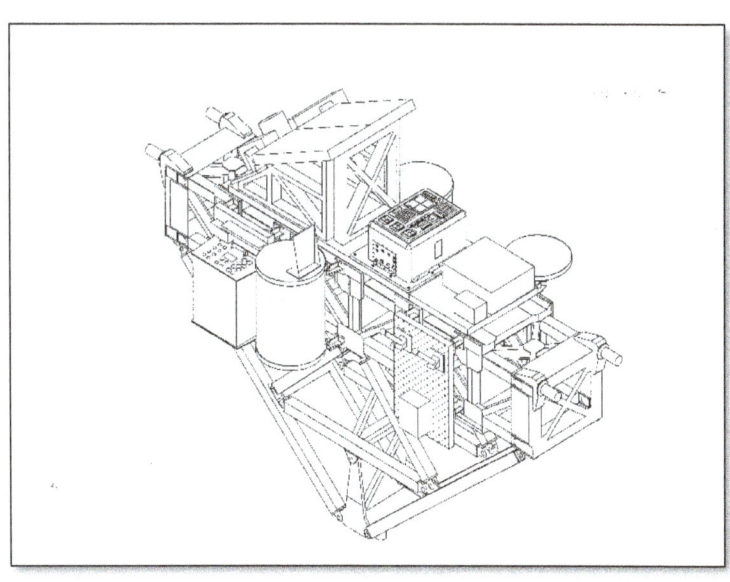

CAD image of SAMPIE onboard the OAST-2 Carrier for mission # STS-62

7004 Aerospace Parkway          Brook Park, Ohio 44142          216.977.1000     Fax 216.977.1269

July 12, 1994

Mr. Harold L. Baker

Dear Mr. Baker:

Mr. Larry Wald, Space Experiments Division, has advised me
that the Solar Array Module Plasma Interaction Experiment
(SAMPIE) Project Team of which you are a member, is to be
commended for their exceptional effort and dedication beyond the
basic requirements of Task 6723.

It is my sincere pleasure to join in acknowledging your
accomplishments.  I would like to add my personal thanks and
congratulations for a job well done.

Sincerely,

Dr. Guion S. Bluford
SETAR Program Manager

/rc

Enclosure

cc:
Michael Korba
William McKissock
Personnel File

Letter of commendation from the first Black astronaut, Dr. Guion
Bluford, for the mechanical component and system design I contributed
to the SAMPIE project.

November 29, 1994

Mr. Harold Baker
XXXXXXXXXXXXXXXXXXX
XXXXXXXXXXXXXXXX

Dear Mr. Baker:

It is my sincere pleasure to give recognition to you for your outstanding performance in support of the μSCaLE project. Your exceptional effort and dedication as a member of the μSCaLE team has made a significant contribution to the research of many fluid physics projects.

I would like to add my personal thanks and congratulations for a job well done. NYMA's ability to meet customer needs is totally dependent on employees like yourself.

Sincerely,

Dr. Guion S. Bluford
SETAR Program Manager

/rc

cc:
Michael Korba
William McKissock
SETAR News
Personnel File

Letter of commendation from Dr. Guion Bluford for the mechanical component and system design I contributed to the Microscale Hydrodynamics Study (μSCALE).

Now, through my work as a design consultant and prototype manufacturer, I have a 3D printing farm where I have produced hundreds of items for a range of client companies, direct sales, home use, and other purposes. I have printed toys for my children, tools for myself, and products to sell. In fact, I will share our custom designed, 3D printed Nguzo Saba themed items in an upcoming section.

42

These efforts have allowed me to live a stable middle-class life, but there is great wealth to be shared in their broader application. There are countless other ideas and possibilities, too.

## III. Essential Kawaida STEM Criticisms

Throughout his career, Dr. Karenga's writings have been a source of relentless criticism of every crime, simple ill deed, or bad thought committed by the dominant culture or ruling class. His criticisms are extensive and laser focused in multiple directions simultaneously. The uncompromising analysis and indisputable clarity have offered those who oppress no relief.

As mentioned, Kawaida STEM criticisms emerge from the Kemetic / Maatian tradition of *"courageous questioning"* – which has been a fundamental principle of Kawaida since its introduction during the 1960's Black Freedom Movement. Looking back, Karenga explains how –

*"Ours was a deliberate and depthful questioning concerning ourselves and then society and the people who ruled it... The questioning was a total questioning, a questioning about how we live, the conditions of our lives, the possibilities of freedom and flourishing, and the unavoidable requirements for achieving them. We questioned the rationality, rightness and sanity of allowing our oppressor to be our teacher or tutor, or to tell us without challenge the tall tales of bringing us civilization and God and saving us from ourselves. We questioned and rejected his claim of being in any way superior; God-sent or possessing some racial or religious right to conquer, kill, dispossess, enslave and oppress us and other peoples of the world. We questioned and rejected his racial and religious claims to be singularly chosen, elect and exalted above all the other peoples of the world. And we refused to let the oppressors interpret and have God as an ally of enslavement, an enabler of holocaust, and a racialized divinity doing the barbaric bidding of the oppressor."* [12]

This level of *courageous questioning* has produced a long list of dominant culture criticisms in Dr. Karenga's writings. I limit my detailed review, here, to criticisms of STEM based activities, most broadly, as it concerns the environment for two reasons.

First, because extreme harm or destruction of natural processes and resources of the environment that gives us life on this planet is the most outrageous and unconscionable of all abuses. Second, because my purpose is to stay focused on us, primarily, and our productive capacities.

I have included an itemized list of other ideas and practices criticized in Karenga's writings to give a sense of the scope and scale of *courageous questioning* related to Kawaida STEM more broadly. But all truly moral people should have our own ample list of criticisms of unethical dominant society values and practices including at least some of the same things.

In his article titled, <u>Repairing and Remaking the World: An Environmental Vision of Justice</u>, Dr. Karenga shares pointed, scathing criticism of dominant culture attitudes and behavior related to applied STEM for our review here.

In this excerpt, he begins laying the basis for his further comments by suggesting that a humble reevaluation of our place in the universe is essential toward addressing degradation of the world caused by reckless and abusive use and application of STEM. He writes –

*"Surely, a rightful approach to the environment begins with rethinking our relationship with the world, our place in it, our obligation towards it and the cost, casualties and future-diminishing consequences of our current deadly course and the thinking and practices which undergird and inform it."* [11]

The text continues asserting that a profound arrogance informs the dominant culture's attitude and behavior toward the world, and each of us must ask ourselves a few related questions about the insanity of it all to help inform our steps forward, saying –

> "We must question the human-centered arrogance that led to the self-assigning of humans, in the name of God, gun and the questionable good of 'man', the right to dominate, tread down, and relentlessly exploit the earth. And we must ask ourselves in earnest what real or hidden reasons, latent logic or simple self-saving common sense is there in knowingly destroying the basis for life on the planet, including our own and that of future generations?" [11]

Karenga closes this excerpt by asking a fundamental question about the abject insanity of using STEM for ultimate self-destruction, writing –

> "In a word, what is the nature and need of the vulgar materialism, social madness and moral numbness that allow us to practice ecocide without considering, caring about or taking serious its sure and certain implications for human genocide?" [11]

While resulting environmental destruction is one of the most extreme consequences of deformed and unprincipled use of STEM, there are many other examples indicated by the varied ways human beings are murdered, oppressed, and/or exploited by immoral use of STEM. Examples of other spiritually deformed practices related to STEM criticized and condemned by Kawaida doctrine include –

a) the general misuse and abuse of STEM for reckless profiteering causing destruction of nature (Ntr) and the diminishing and oppression of human life and possibility
b) environmentally destructive energy systems – nuclear and fossil fuels (coal, oil, natural gas)
c) extreme and unprincipled efforts in the biotechnology sphere that violate all premises of morality and medical ethos to do no harm

45

d)  perpetual warmongering and misuse of STEM to violate and kill people in mass
e)  rewriting of history / deformation and denial of the historical record of technology
f)  purposeful disruption of global creative capacity and diminished capacity in this country

## IV.  Essential Kawaida STEM Challenges

Applied Kawaida STEM values includes challenges and related prohibitions for the population at large, global governments, officials with power and influence, plus corporations who so often define patterns of consumption and production while directing the public agenda.

The challenges detailed here are extracted from the Million Man March Day of Absence Mission Statement (MMM/MS) as written by Dr. Karenga in his leadership capacity on the national organizing committee. This text has broad and varied implications for a Kawaida STEM ethos.

### a.  The challenge to ourselves

The individual and collective challenges posed by Kawaida STEM ethics do not apply exclusively to those who embrace Kawaida ethics. These challenges also apply to all who regard themselves to be upright human beings, grounded in a desire for a good and meaningful life for themselves and others, with due regard for the world around us.

As Karenga explains in the MMM/MS –

*"We understand that the challenge to ourselves is the greatest challenge. For it is only by making demands on ourselves that we can make successful demands on society."* [4]

As it concerns STEM, our challenge includes necessary atonement for failing to uphold our history as creators and innovators of STEM, our moral failures for any active role we have played in STEM related efforts that betray our values for money or other rewards, and our failure to relentlessly challenge the dominant society in all its deformed uses and applications for STEM. This atonement must include a rigorous and diligent commitment to correct these failures and oversights to prevent further negative impact by developing ourselves and engaging society as indicated here. In this way –

*"Atonement means being always concerned about standing worthy before the Creator, before others and before the creation, being humble enough to admit mistakes and wrongs, and bold enough to correct them."* [4]

Beyond that, as it concerns STEM, we mean atonement for not recognizing ourselves as the originators of STEM remade, capable of resisting as needed, and learning to act with authority as both innovators and a moral vanguard for STEM development locally and beyond. We must also atone for accepting less-than-divine perceptions of us as our own, and –

*"... for failing to do as much as we can to protect and preserve the environment through practicing and struggling for environmentally friendly patterns of consumption and production..."* [4]

This includes failing to adequately resist all efforts to entice us to become gross and thoughtless consumers, assume massive debt, or give in to any other unprincipled or unbalanced thing related to products or dollars, or to gain unfair advantage or negatively affect other people in any type of interpersonal, business, or community exchange.

This also includes failing to rise above conditioned acceptance of what Dr. Karenga calls *"the catechism of impossibilities,"* [7 – p.8] which diminishes, at a minimum, and sometimes fully suspends or destroys our people's perception of what is possible.

Of course, we wouldn't be here if Dr. Karenga had allowed anyone to convince him it would be impossible to create a new African social philosophy and to lead creation of a new cultural holiday almost sixty years ago. The fact that he did so despite doubters and naysayers should be enough to inspire those who understand and appreciate Kawaida to believe we can do anything, too.

The applied intent of this <u>Challenge to Ourselves</u> is for us to fully reconcile ourselves with our shortcomings and to correct our course so that we can fully realize ourselves. As it concerns STEM, this means to bring ourselves *"into harmony with the Creator, others,* [and] *creation"* through righteous efforts to fulfill all due responsibilities involved with developing and applying STEM.

To fully meet this obligation, we have to think of ourselves as nothing short of being the Great Pyramid designers and builders reborn.

## b. The challenge to governments

A central principle of fulfilling responsibilities in Kawaida STEM ethics *"is holding responsible those in power who have oppressed and wronged us* [and the world] *through various challenges,"* including immoral and unethical STEM development and use. In the MMM/MS Karenga shares insights that further apply to Kawaida ethics for STEM, saying –

*"We call on the government to also atone for spending more money on imprisonment than education, and on weapons of war than social development; for dismantling regulations that restrained corporations in their degradation of the environment; and for failing to check a deadly environmental racism that encourages placement of toxic waste in communities of color. And of course, we call for a halt to all of this."*

*"Furthermore,* [as it concerns all things STEM related,] *we call on the government... to provide universal, full and affordable health care; to adopt an economic bill of rights including a plan to rebuild the*

*wasting cities; [and] to craft and institute policies to preserve and protect the environment."* [4]

Kawaida STEM ethics challenges us and governments at every level and in every way to act in full authority as protectors of the public interests to use and develop STEM efforts, law, and policy that conforms to those interests, and specifically does not oppose them. We call on the government, particularly, to rightfully restrain corporations and to refrain from all further harmful practices involving STEM. Instead, we call on U.S. and world governments to invest in active efforts of *serudj ta* and other ongoing efforts to prevent further harm and destruction to people or the environment.

## c. The challenge to corporations

The MMM/MS outlines a challenge to corporations detailing the righteous commitments and corrections Kawaida STEM ethics requires for current and future STEM development and application. The text begins by rejecting the common perception –

*"... that corporations have no social responsibility except to maximize profit [in a] competitive market through cutting costs... and constantly increasing technological efficiency. Our position is that no human conduct is immune from the demands of moral responsibility or exempt from moral assessment."* [4]

Dr. Karenga continues by lamenting the vast and extreme impact corporations have on society and how their deformed focus on profit leads to –

*"... harmful products projected as beneficial, environmental degradation, deindustrialization... and disinvestment in social structures and development."* [4]

This leads to further demands that corporations take –

49

*"... responsibility that requires and encourages efforts to minimize and eventually eliminate harmful consequences which persons, communities and the environment sustain as a result of productive and consumptive practices..."* [4]

This challenge makes focused demands for Black communities, particularly where Black communities are the profit base. These include increased investment in public schools and universities, particularly HBCUs – and new investment in *"community institutions and projects"* that promote development in every way.

This should include community-based STEM training programs and enrichment efforts that promote and engage youth interests and talents in STEM, along with other efforts to *"halt and reverse urban decay."* But no effort to benefit the Black community would be complete, and no demand for balanced and reciprocal investment could be met without corporations creating a *"massive job training [initiative in the Black community] for work in the 21st century."* This, by necessity, must include special attention to STEM related fields.

This challenge to corporations closes with a demand for –

*"... corporations to show appropriate care and responsibility for the environment; to minimize and halt pollution, deforestation and depletion of natural resources, and the destruction of plants, animals, birds, fish, reptiles and insects and their natural habitats; and to rebuild wasted and damaged areas and expand the number, size, and kinds of areas preserved."* [4]

This reflects the primary regard for the environment and natural world demonstrated throughout Dr. Karenga's writings from his earliest Kawaida texts through the most recent. It also reflects the need for highly trained, morally grounded specialists in every field and endeavor to emerge among those of us committed to Kawaida STEM ethos to achieve these goals.

50

**D. Goals – Kawaida Distinctions and Desired Outcomes for STEM Development**

**I. Essential Distinctions of Kawaida STEM**

Kawaida STEM ethics distinguishes itself in at least two meaningful ways as compared to the values behind STEM development in this society and the world today. The principal difference is that Kawaida STEM is an African ethos that focuses on developing and using STEM for purposes consistent with the greatest good for the greatest number of people and the environment, as traditional African cultures broadly advance. That is an absolute departure from the profit-and-domination pursuits that drive STEM development today.

Kawaida STEM is also different because, like Kawaida more broadly, it aspires to inspire as many people as possible to become the best version of themselves in a moral, spiritual, or universal sense. There is no interest in suppressing or diminishing the talents or contributions of anyone in Kawaida STEM ethics. Instead, the focus is on elevating the necessary moral and ethical focus involved toward the best possible outcomes as a critically needed departure from increasingly negative consequences being generated by the current approach.

**II. Desired Outcomes for Kawaida STEM**

We will have achieved success and the appropriate outcomes in our efforts toward applied STEM development when either of the follow conditions are brought forth by the related effort:

1. When the greatest possible good has been served for the greatest possible number of people and the world around us; when Maat (righteousness) has been restored

2. When these efforts achieve the goals and objective of the ancient Kemetic and Kawaida concept of *"serudj ta"* which calls for human beings to constantly repair, remake, and improve the world

3. When moral wisdom adequate to govern the world and sustain its existence prevails in leadership roles

This reflects the highest possible moral and ethical aspirations that would be difficult to measure, except by the works produced and outcomes achieved by a given society over time. This is consistent with the human practice of developing and defining morality and spiritual ethics in a way that promotes continuous pursuit of human perfection as an active and ongoing journey, as opposed to being an absolute destination.

The desired outcomes for African people on the continent and throughout the Diaspora generally include the creation and building of new STEM facilities and initiatives to house, develop, and expand our highest STEM aspirations. That goal is an essential step toward the restoration of our self-understanding as pioneers, innovators, and principled users of STEM in a way that assists the overall project of *"rescuing and reconstructing our history and humanity to shape them in our own image and interests."* [16]

### 3) Added Insights and Further Consideration on Kawaida Philosophy and Modern Technology

As mentioned in the introduction, my planned contribution to the Kawaida Work Group Project included a two-part paper where I would extract teachings specific to STEM from Kawaida writings in part one, then write whatever I thought was relevant to Kawaida STEM in part two. This caused me to think broadly about my experience with Kawaida and how my work as a STEM professional always influenced how I perceived it.

I thought about the day, Dr. Karenga mentioned in class that he liked "idea people," or people with their own independent thoughts and ideas about things. I smiled to myself thinking about some of the independent ideas I already had related to what I was learning from him. During that class, he also shared his experience as he earned his second Ph.D. to teach how we can grow and develop by presenting our ideas in settings where they will be critically challenged.

Those lessons align with the Kawaida practice of courageous questioning, where the most meaningful practice of it begins with "*a total questioning* [of ourselves], *a questioning about how we live, the conditions of our lives, the possibilities of freedom and flourishing, and the unavoidable requirements for achieving them.*" [12]

I engage this project through the lens of courageous questioning, and I offer some of these perspectives in that applied spirit. I begin with a brief look back on where this work began for me, leading to the moment I recognized the scale and magnitude of Kawaida with a discussion about why I embrace and advance its teachings. I then address Kawaida and modern technology in various ways, including Kawaida STEM as an Nguzo Saba initiative before closing with an outlook on the future for Kawaida, Kwanzaa, the Nguzo Saba, Black people, and the world.

## A. The Limits of Kawaida Have Not Been Set and Can Not Be Reached – My Perceptions

### The Path to My First Full Kawaida Encounter – The Answer We All Need

My life began almost exactly one year before Dr. King was assassinated. His energy lingered and remained so strong in the neighborhood where I grew up in Detroit that I was inspired to begin studying and writing about him as soon as I began learning to study and write. By second grade I was writing about his life.

I continue to be a student of Dr. King's teachings today, but in the eleventh grade I read "The Autobiography of Malcolm X" for the first time. Like many people, I was so deeply moved by lessons learned from his story that I have read the book several times since – in some ways like a sacred text. My studies of Malcolm X have influenced my thinking over the years more than any other teacher, especially the ideas he shared right before, during, and after his trip to Mecca in April 1964.

By the time I was introduced to Dr. Karenga and Kawaida philosophy as I reached my late thirties, I had been what I describe as "a committed Malcolmist" for two decades. At that point, I had merged my own reasoning with Min. Malcolm's most evolved teachings to conclude that Black people had one major problem that presented itself in a variety of ways - we are overly influenced by *"other people's propaganda."* [14 – p.373]

The truth is, hype and misinformation about history, politics, religion, and other aspects of human life has had a broadly limiting impact on Black people's *"identity, purpose, and direction"* for quite some time. Because of that, we have not yet seen enough within ourselves to do what only we can do to fully realize ourselves and create the world we want and deserve to live in.

To me, race ideology was the main villain – and I had come to think Black people were in a unique position to do something about it, if only we would get *"tired of dealing with other people's propaganda,"* like Min. Malcolm did.

## Understanding Kawaida

I was taking my second class with Dr. Karenga at CSU Long Beach in Fall 2005 (Ancient Egyptian Ethical Thought) when I first began to understand the scope and potential of Kawaida.

With over twenty years' design engineering experience at that point, I had an expansive technical imagination, but the idea of creating a social philosophy was completely foreign to me. I soon realized Kawaida was conceived to be the kind of thought system societies are built around – like socialism, communism, or even democracy – except Kawaida is grounded in African ethical thought.

For many reasons, I thought that was exactly what our people needed – a new way to think about and understand ourselves based on communal African values instead of divisive and exploitive "every man, woman, and child for themselves" type of thinking.

I thought we need a disciplined and balanced mode of thinking that builds protections around the "ethics of sharing" or the spirit of Ubuntu – I am because we are – that distinguish African thought and humanity from the spirit that dominates western culture and the world.

I believe Black people need a modern thought system grounded in the best of African teachings – that can be reduced to a daily code of conduct to show us how to win against all enemies and challenges, internal and external. Like other cultures, we need a roadmap to guide us to become the best possible versions of ourselves, so we can inspire the same in the world around us along the way. In other words, a thought system for a new or improved society inspired by the best of what we and our ancestors can offer – because the world follows us when we're at our best.

I already knew and respected that Kawaida translates to mean – great tradition or a new understanding of what's normal based on great tradition. I also deeply respected how Kawaida is based in the best of African thought, history, and culture – but calls on every generation to improve or add to it – and how Kawaida calls on all people *"to struggle to bring good into the world, and not let any good be lost."* [5,16]

I also liked the sound of the word, Kawaida, and how its vibrant tones often lead people who hear it for the first time to ask the magic question – *"What is Kawaida?"*

When the question is asked, where it leads is entirely up to the person responding in the moment, the way they respond, and the tools they have to aid the effort. The more vast, appealing, and readily available the tools, the better we can share and receive the lessons and benefits of Kawaida for our people and our struggle to create a good world.

Kawaida offers a roadmap to enhance African people's appreciation for our culture, and to reconnect those displaced from it in the most meaningful way. All we have to do is follow the path to gain the knowledge it represents. The fact that we are encouraged and expected to add to its depth and meaning along the way makes it more important for us, establishing limits that can never be set or reached.

The popularity of Kwanzaa and the potential to expand focus on the Nguzo Saba / Seven Principles beyond the seven-day holiday inspired many thoughts about how these teachings needed to be more widely shared.

So as the picture became increasingly clear about what Kawaida really is, and the depth of thought behind it, I became more impressed with it and with Dr. Karenga for conceiving it.

That was the day I began to see Kawaida as *"the code"* our people need. That was also the day I began thinking about the many ways modern technology could be used to teach Kawaida to Black people who have not yet reconnected with Africa. I was beginning to see unlimited potential in Kawaida as a primary tool to help restore our people and create a good world in the best way – by us becoming the best version of ourselves and a model of what we would want to see in other people.

I also realized that with my technical skills, I could make a meaningful contribution to the effort, and I was willing to do it. Not for fame or fortune, but for the good that would come to our people and the world from merging modern technology more expansively with Kawaida.

I was also excited because I was beginning to understand more and more how Kawaida is considered by some to be an extension of Min. Malcolm's work because of its Black socio-political orientation, its grounding in African history and culture, and deep, critical thought. As a committed Malcolmist since I first read his autobiography in the eleventh grade, that was a big thing for me, too, but I had one concern.

## From Malcolmism to Kawaida Advocacy

I came to Kawaida as a committed Malcolmist, convinced by his post-Mecca teachings and my own reasoning that Black people's primary problems all result from various forms of propaganda and our attachments to it. I was convinced that race ideology – the myth that human beings exist as subspecies divided and characterized primarily by skin color – is our biggest problem and one of the most successful propaganda campaigns ever conceived. With Black people designated as the lowest form of human life as a result, race-based thinking has negatively impacted every aspect of our lives creating diminished perceptions of our identity, purpose, and direction.

Religious propaganda has negatively impacted us, as well, by causing far too many of us to disavow our innate spirituality and direct connection to the divine to look toward the sky or outside of ourselves for solutions instead of finding them in the mirror or the collective efforts of our people.

Political propaganda adds to the confusion, too, as we repeatedly trust politicians and the political process to protect or advance our interests even though they repeatedly fall short of the most basic or most meaningful goals.

In this way, religious and political propaganda contributes to us not being able to see enough within ourselves to solve the problems race ideology and American racism created for us. Still, I believe that if we knew better, we would do better.

Because of this, Min. Malcolm's advice about the need for oppressed people to evolve beyond all forms of propaganda – including race-based propaganda – was central to my perspective as a forward strategy. The fact that we face the same race-based challenges after decades and centuries of race-based struggle strongly indicates a new strategy is needed, because doing the same things over again while expecting new and better outcomes is insanity.

Plus, it is a logical contradiction, in many ways, to continue fighting against racism while embracing and advancing race ideology or the race-based thinking that precedes and informs racism. That's like trying to use flames to put out a fire – or a water hose to stop a flood – explaining why it has not yet worked.

With that, in pursuit of race-based objectives, we have been challenged continuously by the question – "Why can't all Black people get along?" That question typically remains unanswered, but Kawaida offers us a perspective. Our unity around Blackness has been challenged, at least in part, because we don't have a shared, elevated conception of what it means to be Black. To demonstrate this, we only need to ask a dozen or more Black people – *"What does it mean to be Black?"* – to consider our related thoughts.

Beyond references to skin color and African origins that are not exclusive to us, responses will range from a blank stare – with no response at all – to a variety of common perceptions, stereotypes, and references to our experience with oppression being shared. Some will respond with comments about what Black people think, or what Black people have contributed to human history, but not enough. Still, the answers will vary enough to demonstrate why unity in practice is impossible without unity in thought, as Sun Tzu and many other strategic thought leaders teach. [27]

So, in comments made at Harvard on March 18, 1964, Min. Malcolm laid a foundation for the new ideas he would share in a series of letters from Mecca in the weeks to come by calling for new ideas. On this day at Harvard, he voiced support for Elijah Muhammad's ideas on racial separation. But within two months he would share a new belief that oppressed people need to evolve beyond the propaganda of race-based thinking altogether to win the battle against racism.

Early in his remarks at The Leverett House Forum, Malcolm declared that oppressed people were no longer *"looking toward the oppressor [for a] system of logic or reason."* To that, he added *"What is logical [and reasonable] to the oppressor isn't logical [and reasonable] to the oppressed. There just has to be a new system of reason and logic devised by us who are at the bottom, if we want to get some results in this struggle called 'the [Black] Revolution.'"* [15 – p.133]

Realizing how desperate we were for new ideas to help solve the race problem, Min. Malcolm explained how his new organization *"places an accent on youth."* Then adding –

*"We are issuing a call for students across the country, from coast to coast, to launch a new study of the problem – not a study that is in any way guided or influenced by adults, but a study of their own. Thus, we can get a new analysis of the problem, a more realistic analysis. After this new study and more realistic analysis, we are going to ask those same students for a new approach to the problem."* [15 -p.143]

Min. Malcolm went on to say some of the new ideas young people were already offering created the potential for *"a new era here in this country."* He repeated that *"we are issuing a call to youth, primarily, to get some new ideas and a new direction."* Because, *"The adults,"* he said, *"are more confused than the problem itself. It will take a whole generation of new people to approach* [and fix] *this problem."* [15 – p.156]

Just a few short weeks later, and as written in The Autobiography of Malcolm X, Min. Malcolm began explaining that it was not only possible, but necessary, to evolve past race-based propaganda in a series of letters he sent to family, friends, and associates during his trip to Mecca.

He introduces the idea in the chapter titled "1965," where he declared –

*"My thinking had been opened up wide in Mecca. In the long letters I wrote to friends, I tried to convey to them my new insights into the American black man's struggle and his problems, as well as the depths of my search for truth and justice.*

*"I've had enough of someone else's propaganda,' I had written to these friends. I'm for truth, no matter who tells it. I'm for justice, no matter who it is for or against. I'm a human being first and foremost,*

*and as such I'm for whoever and whatever benefits humanity as a whole."* [14 – p.373]

That chapter – and the two before it – are full of lamentations about our struggle against racism and his evolving thoughts, particularly on the racist confusion created in the world by some of the most highly destructive social propaganda ever conceived by *"someone else"* – race ideology. These moments reflected a dramatic awakening in Malcolm and his highest point of moral evolution in my opinion. It is unfortunate that his new perspectives were rejected by even his most faithful followers then and today.

### The Origins of Kawaida Philosophy

At the same time these events unfolded for Min. Malcolm, Maulana Karenga was pursuing his college and graduate studies in Los Angeles and laying a foundation for the African centered cultural and social change philosophy he would call, Kawaida. He was and is a student of Min. Malcolm's teachings, and is among the scholars recognized and respected for protecting and helping to cultivate Min. Malcolm's legacy by his family and the conscious community. Min. Malcolm's teachings always have been and continue to be primary inspiration for Kawaida.

In fact, Dr. Karenga interpreted Min. Malcolm's call for *"a new system of reason and logic"* to defeat racism as a call for *"a new language and logic"* based in *"tradition and reason"* that would present itself as a necessary and natural better alternative to reasonable people who hear of it. The inspiration from Malcolm to create *"a new language and logic"* has been a core principle and pursuit of Kawaida.

Yet, in seeming contrast to Min. Malcolm's call for *"a new system of reason and logic"* to counter and ultimately replace the propaganda of race ideology, Kawaida philosophy forcefully projects *"unbudging Blackness"* as a permanent foundation and operational strategy. This comes as no surprise considering Dr. Karenga was a leading theorist of the 1960's Black Power Movement and continues to be a Black

Nationalist thought leader through ongoing teaching and writing efforts. [7 – p.15]

A potential response to this is to note that Kawaida distinguishes its conception of Blackness from the broadly accepted race idea by presenting Blackness as a structured, broad-based, uniquely organized, and highly elevating cultural concept. Blackness in the Kawaida tradition is far more expansive than limited, race-based ideas advanced through negative stereotypes suggesting we have no meaningful history before enslavement and make no greater consistent contribution to society than sports and entertainment.

In response to this, the central thesis of Kawaida since its inception has been to assert that –

*"The key crisis in Black life is a cultural crisis; a crisis of views and values affecting the way we see ourselves in the world, and the values that inform the way we engage it."*

In Kawaida, culture is the foundation of everything. All challenges faced in Black communities can be characterized as a problem related to our chosen, inherited, or imposed culture, and all solutions to those challenges can also be found through culture.

Dr. Karenga explains –

*"In Kawaida philosophy, culture is understood as a unique and equally valuable way of being human in the world. Thus, each people has the right and responsibility to live and express their own unique and equally valid and valuable way of being human in the world. African peoples are thus called to do likewise as both a requirement for struggle and an indispensable method of enriching and expanding their lives. Within this overarching framework, culture is the fundamental context in which a person and people understand and assert themselves, in a word, the fundamental source of their identity, purpose, and direction.*

*Here Kawaida calls for and poses its own project as a continuous dialog with African culture. To dialog with African culture is to ask it questions and seek from it answers to the fundamental and enduring concerns of the African and human community. These include questions of – identity, purpose, and direction; meaning and mission in human life; the grounds for a just and good society; our obligation to others; a framework for a rightful relationship with the environment; and the basis of human freedom and human flourishing and its role in the liberation struggle itself. Again, <u>at the heart of this conversation with African culture is the continuing quest to define and become the best of what it means to be African and human in the fullest sense</u>.*" [9 – p.262]

Dr. Karenga further explains that Kawaida responds directly to Min. Malcolm's call for "*a new system of reason and logic*" by "*creating a language and logic of liberation, offering both opposition and affirmation, i.e., opposing oppression and affirming the people.*" Within this framework, we find a uniquely well-conceived, multi-layered conception of Blackness that is purposefully elevating for all who embrace it.

Because I have studied Kawaida, I understood the depth and significance of its definition of culture and of Blackness as a cultural concept compared to a racial idea. Kawaida asserts there are seven fundamental aspects to culture –

"*...spirituality and ethics (religion); history; social organization; economic organization; political organization; creative production (art, music, literature, dance, etc.); and ethos – the collective psychology shaped by activities in the other six areas.*" [9 – p.261]

Most recently, Kawaida defines the three core components of Blackness to be – "*culture, consciousness, and committed practice.*" For me, that means I am informed about and committed to my Pan African culture; I am conscious of and committed to fulfilling the expectations my culture establishes for me as a man among our people in the world; and I am committed on a continuous, daily, nonstop basis to living the values of my culture and building the relationships and community that will protect, sustain, and help develop our people and culture and the world around us into the future.

In a prior construct, Kawaida defined the three core components of Blackness to be – *"color, culture, and consciousness."* I believe replacing *"color"* with *"committed practice"* here was consistent with Malcolm's admonition to evolve beyond race, consistent with African teachings, and also consistent with Kawaida's expressed intent to project a *"new language and logic"* for two reasons.

First, because Black people come in every shade and skin color under the Sun, color, alone, is not as much a distinguishing feature as we may perceive.

Second, and more importantly, skin color quickly fades as a legitimate concern in the presence or absence of committed practice. Meaning, that when certain Black people's practice conflicts with our community's best interests, their skin color only matters as a descriptive reference to locate them and address their behavior, or as a debilitating emotional attachment when their behavior is not addressed.

### The Paradox of Talking Black

I understand the depths of Kawaida and its expansive presentation of Blackness as a cultural concept because I have studied it for many years. But since the language of Blackness as a cultural concept sounds just like Blackness as a racial idea from a distance, I knew the masses could and often would miss the deeper understanding until they get close enough to learn the difference.

Because of this, I was convinced the most revolutionary things about Kawaida would be consistently missed as the language of *"unbudging Blackness"* is understandably received as race-based thinking as compared to what I perceive it to be, at its best – a complete replacement for race-based thinking by those wilingl to embrace its focus on applied values and committed practice, instead.

Imagine the difference in the Black community and the world if Black people increasingly align our conception of Blackness with committed practice instead of skin color. We would certainly be moving past the propaganda of race ideology as Min. Malcolm advised us to do over fifty years ago. Surely, the world would be a better place because of it. The world would follow us, too, then, because we would be at our best.

But since we were just learning to say "I'm Black and I'm proud" back then, Malcolm's new ideas were not well received by the masses. It was interesting how the media didn't receive Malcolm's new teachings very well, either, but for different reasons.

### Learning to Understand the New Language and Logic in Kawaida's "Unbudging Blackness"

Since I had been committed to Min. Malcolm's post Mecca teachings for decades, and was newly inspired by the cultural and social change philosophy, Kawaida, I found it necessary to fully address my concerns with the conflict that could be perceived between Min. Malcolm's post Mecca advice and Kawaida's "*unbudging Blackness.*"

It is important to note I was never hostile to Blackness. Not at all. Instead, with Min. Malcolm's - "*By any means necessary*" – dictate in mind, along with what Kawaida teaches about critical self-assessment, "*courageous questioning,*" and the creative power of words, it was a worthwhile and necessary exercise. The outcome led to a full merger between Malcolm's final teachings and Kawaida, and a renewed energy towards proposing that merger as a forward strategy with all the tools of modern technology.

But since Min. Malcolm's call for us to evolve beyond race ideology was not well received by the Black masses at all back then, I was reasonably concerned the idea would also be rejected today. Even among those who had been drawn to his words for over a decade before, there was collective reluctance toward – if not immediate rejection of – his new teachings. Malcolm understood that, too. He even anticipated it. He knew this was a significantly different perspective. Plus, he knew his people.

But Malcolm also found it interesting that –

"...*the American white man's press refused to convey that* [he] *was now attempting to teach* [Black people] *a new direction.*" [14 – p.373]

That makes perfect sense, too, because race ideology is working as intended for some segments of the population, including those who own all the major media outlets, and they wouldn't want that disturbed.

I think I would have rejected his new perspective back then, too. I didn't embrace it during my first few readings of the autobiography. But now, well over fifty years after he shared his new perspective, I can understand why he began to see things as he did. Race propaganda has been mostly all bad news for our people. No one can deny that.

Plus, there is the logical contradiction of identifying with and advancing race ideology while trying to deconstruct racism when race ideology precedes and informs racism. Think about that...

I have the benefit of hindsight today, and Kawaida requires I use it in my own critical reasoning. There should be no doubt that race ideology is our enemy, but how do we engage that idea against the reality that Black people love being Black?

When Malcolm returned from Mecca in 1964 with these new perspectives, our people were becoming increasingly comfortable with Blackness as a revolutionary identity, newly described in positive, self-affirming terms with powerful imagery, language, and music that was distinctly different compared to the way Blackness had been perceived and portrayed before then. Because of this, Malcolm struggled with his conception of this idea, and ran out of time before he was able to resolve it.

I had become convinced that a merger between Kawaida and Min. Malcolm's teachings will adequately reflect both *"a new system of reason and logic"* and *"a new language and logic"* that would not only represent a meaningful response to the propaganda of race ideology, but an effective replacement for it in practice.

A highly unlikely meeting with the vice president of Min. Malcolm's Organization for Afro-American Unity (OAAU) in July 2015 helped me figure out what that should look like.

## My July 2015 Meeting with the Vice President of Min. Malcolm's Organization of Afro-American Unity (OAAU)

I wrote my first paper on my struggle between Min. Malcolm's teachings against race ideology and Kawaida's *"unbudging Blackness"* while I was in my second class with Dr. Karenga. I shared the paper with him, but it wasn't an assignment for his class. Instead, it was one of many papers I have written over the years to help develop my thoughts in some way, to sometimes share with others for critical dialogue.

Besides encouraging me to read an article he wrote addressing his organization's *"unbudging Blackness,"* Dr. Karenga's only response was to caution me about *"embracing ideas that leave the people out."* I explained that my position *"is centered around the people doesn't leave the people out in any way,"* so I was unable to interpret his remark, and he offered no further clarification. He understood what he meant, though, without explaining any further.

I was stunned by the suggestion that evolving beyond race-based thinking *"leaves [Black] people out."* He seemed to be saying there is no way to understand ourselves except through the lens of race, but I know he knows that is not true. I sought more insight from him, but his *"unbudging Blackness"* had spoken, so I accepted it and looked elsewhere to advance my understanding.

I wrote my last paper on this matter a decade later in 2015, titled The Conversation We Need to Have with Minister Malcolm where I examined his post Mecca teachings and advice about race propaganda. I submitted the paper to the <u>African Heritage Studies Association</u> (AHSA) for presentation at their annual conference held in Long Beach, CA in November 2017, and they accepted it. The study group I directed for more than a decade met in Long Beach thru 2016, so this was all familiar ground for me.

We did very good work in our study group, the <u>Afrikan Restoration Project</u> (ARP), and we enjoyed several remote and live lectures from many prominent Pan African scholars. We also had an active relationship with the <u>Black Student Association</u> at nearby <u>CSU Long Beach</u>, where Dr. Karenga leads the <u>Africana Studies Department</u>. He was an honored lecturer for us, too.

Years before that, in late 2010, we had a different special visitor stop in for one of our sessions. He was a soft-spoken eighty-year-old Black man who I didn't recognize as he approached. But I knew every one of the four Black men surrounding him in formation – Kwesi Osafo, Mathu Ater, Tehuti Kambui, and Okera Damani – each one a warrior and a scholar. I could tell by the way they were moving that he was royalty.

The elderly man who had been escorted to the front row of our study group was Minister Malcolm's close friend and primary colleague, the vice president of the <u>Organization for Afro-American Unity</u> (OAAU), Min. Malcolm's official photographer, the engineer behind many of the audio and video recordings of Min. Malcolm we have all heard, and a "brilliant mathematician," [26] scholar, engineer, and teacher in his own right – the Honorable Prof. Earl 5X Grant.

As a true Malcolmist, I immediately recognized his name when it was whispered to me, as I did an uncontrollable double take. I knew exactly who he was, but I had no idea he was still alive, and I knew nothing about what happened with him after we lost Min. Malcolm. But there he sat in the front row of my study group. I almost couldn't believe it was happening.

As it turned out, Prof. Grant was originally from Los Angeles, and had returned to his hometown many years ago after completing advanced degrees at Harvard and MIT, and after living in Ghana for some time.

According to my friend, Tehuti Kambui, who was his primary colleague –

*"While in Ghana, under the leadership of Dr. Kwame Nkrumah, [Prof. Grant] worked as an engineer at the OAU [Organization of African Unity] Conference Hall until a coup overthrew Nkrumah's government. In 1966, he returned to the USA."* [24]

He was told good things about our study group by one of the four Black men who escorted him in, Okera Damani, and he wanted to see for himself. Our co-director, Brother Kwesi Osafo (may he rest in peace and power) and I were thrilled to learn the next day that Prof. Grant liked what he saw and wanted to come back to our study group to teach. I was honored and truly couldn't believe it was happening.

We were quick to accept his offer. By the time I set up another study group in Pomona in late 2017, Prof. Grant had lectured for us in Long Beach almost a dozen times on a wide range of topics dealing with history, science, and technology. When he found out I was a design engineer, he asked me what I knew about plasma physics, and we had a great talk about it.

I shared that my only point of reference was what I learned about plasma physics while working on my first space flight experiment at NASA. The Solar Array Module Plasma Interaction Experiment (SAMPIE) [21] was a very high-profile space experiment for the NASA Glenn Research Center, which was then known as the NASA Lewis Research Center. The data collected was central to the power system design for the International Space Station (ISS) now on orbit. I enjoyed explaining how SAMPIE was designed to test how different metals would react in the plasma found in Low Earth Orbit (LEO), and which solar cell technology would most efficiently extract electrical energy.

Prof. Grant enjoyed that story and understood every technical aspect of it, then added lessons about plasma as an unlimited energy source that made our talk even more unique than it already was. I hope he enjoyed those talks, too. As a small token of our appreciation, we gave him an honorary doctorate from the community university we claimed as the source of our study group accreditation – the other USC – the <u>University of South Central Los Angeles</u> (USCLA)!

Dr. Earl 5X Grant, as he was then known to us, made a tremendous contribution to our struggle most broadly, and to our study group efforts, specifically. He became an ancestor on my birthday in April 2019, which initially caused me added grief before I decided to see it as a call to action, instead. His spirit filled the memorial service in June 2019, sparking conversations and collaborative efforts that continued his life's work toward elevating Black people in meaningful ways.

Professor Grant – as he was most widely known outside of our study group – was a brilliant man, a true polymath, a modern-day Imhotep who mastered knowledge of different disciplines. I count it as a win that I got to know him well enough to be able to visit his home in July 2015 to get his thoughts on my paper, <u>The Conversation We Need to Have with Minister Malcolm</u> long before I presented it at the 2017 AHSA Conference.

That conversation proved to be truly eye-opening for me. By that time, Dr. Grant was eighty-five years old. He read my paper before I got there, and I had an outstanding ninety-minute conversation with him and Brother Tehuti Kambui. The audio recording of that discussion is a treasured possession.

During our talk, Prof. Grant shared that he thought I understood Min. Malcolm's intent that we should evolve beyond race thinking altogether. But he also shared that Malcolm understood what a complex effort that would be. Brother Tehuti added – "*Malcolm said that he wasn't a racist, but that he <u>was</u> a realist.*" [25] With that, we agreed that Min. Malcolm saw evolving past race as an incremental process, because as Prof. Grant said –

"*We'll get to the African thing, but right now, we gotta stay with the Black thing, because that's the word* [identity] *that fits us over here.*"
[25]

While speaking about African Americans who reconnect meaningfully with African culture, and how racism frames our daily reality whether we reconnect or not, he said –

*"Being African [over here] means that you've taken out time to study a lot of things. But you're abused because you're Black, not because you don't know you're African."* [25]

He commented that Malcolm's perspectives were well ahead of Black people in general and other Black leaders at the time, in particular, and we agreed that most people still haven't caught up. He also acknowledged the need to evolve beyond race identity to fully restore ourselves, but cautioned that something drastic or tragic would have to happen to cause Black people to cancel race-based thinking. In the absence of such an event, another strategy is needed.

My conversation with Dr. Grant helped resolve my concerns with potential conflicts between Min. Malcolm's teachings on ending race-based propaganda and Kawaida's *"unbudging Blackness."* I still believed Min. Malcolm was correct to assert the need to evolve beyond race-based thinking, but I also began to see the importance of Kawaida's *"unbudging Blackness"* more expansively as a required step in that process.

I still believed our embrace of race ideology reflects the highest demonstration of social dominance and conformance to an oppressive system of reason and logic, based, in part, on Dr. Karenga's definition of social power. Here he states – *"The highest demonstration of social power is having the capacity to define reality for others, then cause them to accept it, even when it's to their disadvantage."*

This definition clearly indicates how our embrace of race ideology represents the single *"highest demonstration of* [other people's] *social power"* over us. That's because we know race ideology is false information and propaganda with no basis in biology or reality. Yet, we accept it as truth even though race-based propaganda has been more to our disadvantage than all others.

But also, race ideology is European and American propaganda that departs fully from African ways of understanding ourselves and each other. In this way, our continued embrace violates the often stated Kawaida contention that *"Our oppressor cannot be our teacher."* It also contradicts Min. Malcolm's assertion that *"what is reasonable to the oppressor* [should not be] *reasonable to the oppressed."*

Ultimately, I was concerned that we don't share a common or adequately elevated conception of what Blackness means, making it literally impossible for us to unite around Blackness in a meaningful way. To confirm this, all we must do is ask a good number of Black people what Blackness means to them to allowed the varied answers to prove this point.

As I looked for an elevated conception of Blackness to inform our self-perception and future efforts, I was increasingly troubled that so few organizations offer a definition of what Blackness means or should me to us. Without an adequately elevated and commonly shared self-conception, the sustained level of unity needed around Blackness to create and sustain positive change in our communities and the world is not only challenged, as we have seen, but it may not be possible.

That was when I began to reflect on the expansive meaning of Blackness in Kawaida. That was also when I decided that promoting it among our people was not only a strategy to eventually evolve beyond race-based thinking, but also a meaningful first step toward resolving racism, solving our problems, and becoming the best and fullest version of ourselves.

With this, my concerns about Blackness as a racial idea were addressed by a broader, fuller, and more meaningful presentation of Blackness as a cultural idea. The immediate task, then, for me is to advance the Kawaida conception of Blackness to elevate our self-conception and evolve past *"other people's propaganda"* to move the world in a positive direction like our ancestors and children expect. With that understanding, I recommitted to advancing these teachings as far as my abilities and modern technology allows. Because if we can elevate our self-perception in this way, we become the best version of ourselves, and if we do that, the world will follow us – as it always does when we are at our best.

In that moment I had profound respect and appreciation for Dr. Grant for sharing his insight and for connecting me with Min. Malcolm's perspective in that moment like no one else could. May he rest in peace and power eternally. I also had renewed respect and appreciation for Min. Malcolm having the insight to challenge us to grow and develop ourselves through new ideas. I had greater respect and appreciation for Dr. Karenga's contributions, too, and the *"unbudging Blackness"* in Kawaida, particularly its presentation of Blackness as an expansive cultural concept.

The following pictures are from our study group and my experience with Dr./Prof. Earl 5X Grant.

---

Shujaa Baker and Earl 5X Grant at his home

Bro. Abdullah, Kwesi Osafo, Dr. Grant, Mathu Ater, Shujaa Baker at the Afrikan Restoration Project / Long Beach

| Dr. Earl 5X Grant and Okera Damani (who told him about our study group) | Dr. Grant reviewing Okera's lecture on Malcolm X | Okera Damani holding Canopic Jar with image of Anubis containing Dr. Grant's remains at his memorial |

Dr. Grant with Tehuti Kambui

### Distinguishing Between Blackness as Race or Culture – the Elevated Kawaida Conception of Blackness

The Kawaida conception of Blackness as a cultural idea departs from Blackness as a racial idea in a variety of meaningful ways, beginning with its inception.

Blackness came to exist as a structured racial idea encoded in American policy, law, and society as an extreme counterpart to the introduction of Whiteness as a racial idea in 1681. [30 – p.2] This occurred just five short years after an infamous event called Bacon's Rebellion (1676), where enslaved Africans teamed up with poor and exploited middle class colonists to violently oppose the colonial government, destroying the Jamestown Settlement.

The race concept was then conceived to induce poor and middle-class European American colonists to align with and protect American ruling class interests. As we see in the current political climate, that trick is still working today as poor and working-class people vote against their interests.

Although many people of African descent had long been described as "black" skinned people before this, the concept of Blackness as a formal racial idea originated with this effort. The extreme negative intent and result became immediately clear as the introduction of race ideology coincided with enslavement being made permanent, inheritable, and more brutal for African people held captive.

Because of this, Blackness was constantly ridiculed, where the accepted meaning aligned fully with how we perceive "the N-word" today. Calling someone "Black" was largely considered to be an insult before Blackness was elevated in the 1960s with the introduction of new ideas about Black pride, organized efforts toward Black Power, and more positive presentation of Blackness and Black people in all forms of media.

As noted here, Kawaida came into existence during this period and specifically as a focused effort to elevate Blackness and Black people, consistent with Min. Malcolm's call for *"a new system or reason and logic,"* or as Dr. Karenga interpreted it, *"a new language and logic."* [7 – p.8] I am one among the people who see Kawaida as an example of the *"new system of reason and logic"* Min. Malcolm called for just before he went to Mecca. [15 – p.133]

Kawaida distinguishes itself in this way with its focus on culture as a roadmap to the solutions we need employing *"the best of African*

74

*thought and practice in constant exchange with the world."* The elevated conception of Blackness as a cultural idea extends from that, and departs from the sorely diminished conception of Blackness as a racial idea in a variety of important ways.

First, Blackness as a cultural idea is grounded in Kawaida's expansive interpretation of what culture is and how it is comprised. In this way, the seven fundamental aspects of culture (*spirituality/religion, history, social structure, economic structure, political structure, creative production, and ethos*) establish a broad base to consider who we are that draws from the best of our history and contributions to the human family. This directly contrasts the concept of Blackness as a racial idea designed to diminish Black people's standing and self-concept in the world.

Blackness as a race idea vilifies Africa and discourages or denies any meaningful association between descendant African or Black people and the continent. We see the results of this when we consider how common it is for some Black people to dismiss our efforts to share good news about African history and culture by asking and saying to us –

> *"Why you always talking about that Africa stuff? I'm not African. I'm Black."*

If we then asked these same Black people – "What does it mean to be Black?" – their answer would surely reveal more damage to their self-conception. Countless numbers of Black American or African American people are injured like this, and many can't help but to show it.

In this way, a Black racial identity allows, if not, promotes, rejection of African identity, in favor of a diminished conception of Africanness. It teaches or implies that our history began with enslavement and we are permanently and perpetually relegated to a secondary status, at best, in society.

75

By contrast, Blackness as a cultural identity in Kawaida establishes an immediate and meaningful reconnection with Africa beginning long before White people and other invaders arrived. Kawaida reflects and projects the most elevated and thoughtfully conceived conception of Blackness yet advanced that I am aware of. Distinguishing features include –

- a self-understanding grounded in knowledge that African history did not begin with enslavement, but was interrupted by enslavement
- primary consideration for the best of African thought and cultural practice as a roadmap and direct guide to our full recovery and self-realization
- a principled focus on applied values where Blackness is not only a function of how you look, but also how you engage the community and relate to the world around you
- principled obligations to serve self, community, and the world in the most ethical and effective ways
- constant study and the pursuit of human excellence and self-mastery
- the ultimate need to stand worthy before other people, nature, and the divine
- constant awareness as self-conscious agents of our own liberation and destiny

By contrast, distinguishing features of Blackness as a racial idea include –

- active separation from all things African
- identity and self-concept grounded in the diminished and self-limiting ideas, values, and practices associated with the lowest human status
- active efforts to advance the enslavement period as the beginning of our history
- active encouragement to view ourselves collectively as victims in this society

- active encouragement toward gross materialism and submission to diminished stereotypical behaviors
- promotion of Black people as inherently criminal

Besides those critical distinctions, Kawaida's focus on applied values reflects the criteria human beings actually practice when choosing who we unite with in love, work, service, and struggle. In these relationships, shared interests, values, and goals prevail over our shared heritage, causing our shared race with many people to become, in practice, a point of reference exceeded by higher criteria, and other times a debilitating distraction.

In other words, and in response to the proverbial question – "Why can't all Black people get along?" – the answer is simple. <u>All Black people don't get along, or can't be united in life, service, and struggle simply because all Black people don't share the same values</u>. Regardless of our shared race, heritage, or similar complexions, people ultimately unite around shared values, interests, and goals above all else.

Plus, since it's clear that race ideology is the "race" in racism, it is a logical contradiction to seek to destroy racism while embracing or advancing race ideology.

Ultimately, I think, the applied values focus of Kawaida is the alternative to race-based thinking the world needs. Yet, as a central Black Nationalist philosophy, Kawaida's profound, and, truly revolutionary focus on values as the basis of human understanding and activity is often missed, particularly from a distance, because of limited preconceptions and sometimes disregard or undue fear of Black liberation language, ideas, and objections.

In this way, Kawaida concedes its superior ethical status, unintentionally, by being misconstrued in the context of race ideology, or only as a response to it. Properly understood, Kawaida's focus on applied values should be seen as a righteous and thoughtfully complete replacement for race or color-based thinking.

With that, America is certainly addicted to race ideology as the foundation of racism and the American way of life, and African Americans are strongly addicted, too. If we would begin to recover from our own race addiction by embracing an elevated, applied values based, cultural conception of Blackness, we would become a model to lead the rest of the world to overcoming their race addiction, too.

No other people have as much to gain from this effort as we do, and if we won't do it, who will?

This aligns with our motto for The Afrikan Restoration Project, which states –

*"What you'll do for yourself depends on what you think about yourself. What you think about yourself depends on what you know about yourself. And what you know about yourself begins with what you call yourself. So, who are you, and what does that mean?"*

In my opinion, the Kawaida conception of Blackness offers Black people the best and most complete response to that question available. In that spirit, and from the Kawaida perspective, I'm a Black man, and my Blackness means *"culture, consciousness, and committed practice."*

I ask you, "What does your Blackness mean?" TM

## B. Kawaida and Modern Technology: Current Status, Challenges, and Recommendations

### Current Status of Kawaida Philosophy and Modern Technology

The global popularity of Kwanzaa and the Nguzo Saba / Seven Principles and the many ways that manifests online, in print, and through various broadcast media represents most of the engagement between Kawaida teachings and modern technology. With Dr. Karenga being recognized as a leading scholar of Pan African history and culture, Kawaida is – and will continue to be – actively examined and measured on its merit in the halls of academia with attendant technologies.

Many organizations that celebrate Kwanzaa or use the Nguzo Saba / Seven Principles as part of their operating mission have a variety or related content on the internet and across all social media platforms. The content is plentiful, but also limited to the extent that I found nothing online that uses the most modern and engaging tools and technologies to build on the Black community's familiarity with these teachings.

When my brother, Akhir Rashad, and I began the task of revising The Official Kwanzaa Website in 2017, we proposed dramatic updates to the website that had existed in its original form since it was first developed in 1998 – almost twenty years before. Most of our ideas were not accepted, but we were encouraged to pursue and develop them independently. In 2023 we were inspired to pursue and implement those recommendations with no further delay, as described in an upcoming section.

### Challenges to Using Modern Technology to Advance Kawaida Philosophy

Ultimately, the challenges involved with using modern technology to expand Kawaida's reach and impact speaks to the primary struggle Kawaida engages in *"the battle to win the hearts and minds of our people."* Simply put, far too many Black people either – (1) don't know enough about Kawaida to see its value; or (2) they're not interested *"in all of that Africa stuff;"* or (3) they have been deterred by controversial stories involving Dr. Karenga from the COINTELPRO era.

There are several reasons why we struggle to win the hearts and minds of our people. For every valid reason, there is a distinct response to be developed. Black people have been so greatly influenced by propaganda and misinformation that it can be very difficult to even engage some of us in a discussion about the things Kawaida holds dear – African history and people.

The challenges toward advancing Kawaida begins with the difficulties involved with drawing people's attention to truly useful or quality content in competition with the useless and otherwise distracting content and propaganda being streamed nonstop. Average attention spans are measurably shorter these days, and consistent with that, we live and die with devices attached to our hand or hip these days. With no existing multi-featured apps and virtually no truly engaging multimedia content available online to positively benefit from and use hand held devices and online content in this way, efforts to expand understanding and appreciation for all things Kawaida related are limited.

Besides that, the lingering controversies with Dr. Karenga resulting directly from COINTELPRO activities were designed to create division in the Black community. It is both a sad and unfortunate reality that those efforts still contribute to division within our community today.

NONE OF US should be OK with that – and ALL OF US should be trying to end that influence.

This effect is most clearly demonstrated by the annual practice of certain Black people condemning and speaking against Kwanzaa every year, particularly in the areas surrounding Los Angeles where related events unfolded. That annual chorus was one of my greatest frustrations for more than a decade as I coordinated our community based cultural study group – The Afrikan Restoration Project. Some of these critics do still celebrate Kwanzaa, while being overtly critical of Dr. Karenga as its recognized creator.

As a scholar of ancient and modern African history and ethical thought, I think Dr. Karenga bears primary responsibility for leading our community to a resolution on these matters, and his original translations of ancient African sacred texts provide the necessary guidance. A peace treaty signed in 2022 between the Us Organization and the Black Panther Party San Diego Chapter demonstrates his leadership on this. [28]

To the extent ongoing issues and concerns related to his assault conviction remain unresolved, I maintain that our community bears primary responsibility, then, for healing ourselves on this matter, and for rising above outside manipulations and personality concerns in our best interests.

The chorus of voices opposing Dr. Karenga appear to have been aimed at affecting or limiting his status as a scholar and reputable teacher of Pan African history and ethical thought. Yet, neither those voices – or the issues they are based on – have prevented him from being recognized among the world's most highly acclaimed scholars. That's because the depth and scope of his work to rescue and reconstruct African and Pan African history is worthy of that status.

Those voices also haven't stopped the growth and spread of Kwanzaa, either, which is now celebrated by millions of descendant African people worldwide. But those voices have been successful in causing some Black people to avoid accessing Dr. Karenga's writings and teachings, and the benefits to be gained from them, particularly young people.

Black people who are convinced in this way miss an opportunity to learn critical information about our history – the kind of information central to all perceptions of Black people's identity, purpose, direction, and collective status – from one of our leading scholars, by all objective accounts. By rejecting Kwanzaa, they miss critical opportunities to participate in community building rituals, activities, and ceremonies that build and reinforce the bonds between us.

Also, assuming all related claims are true, they miss an opportunity to better understand those matters in the context in which they occurred, to then hold the people who created that context primarily liable for the inevitable war crimes that occur in the presence of war, and particularly, unjust war.

Perhaps most of all, they miss or dismiss any opportunity or responsibility to effectively explain why mistakes made over fifty years ago should be the basis for dismissing and judging someone who spent years in prison for some of what he has been accused of, followed by fifty-plus years of high-level scholarship with no suggestion of a continuing practice of what he was accused of.

For me and many other people familiar, that represents an example of redemption over time that others could learn from. Particularly, when the whole story is properly understood and adequately explained.

As I look back on the related history and concerns as I approach my senior years, I can easily see how revolutionary minded young people in their twenties were manipulated by COINTELPRO efforts to make the many mistakes that were made during that era. In fact, with all that I know about it now, I'm really surprised that more mistakes weren't made...

I am surprised, too, that we continue to allow these fifty-plus year-old issues to divide us at any level, even as we know that was the original intent. I can only imagine that COINTELPRO's principal architects are somewhere at this very moment smiling – still – while we continue spinning and fighting over the confusion they ultimately caused.

We address these issues in greater detail in writings and blog posts related to our three-year initiative leading up to the 60th Kwanzaa Anniversary in 2026 titled – An Ujima Quest for a Kwanzaa Jubilee. In that effort, we seek to expand understanding of the Kwanzaa creation process by introducing some of the people who assisted Dr. Karenga in that effort. There, we also explain how we addressed our concerns with the controversies involving Dr. Karenga in our study group as we made a conscious choice to continue learning from him. Our Kwanzaa Jubilee campaign is a core part of our broader efforts to merge the teachings of Kawaida with modern technology in a way that hasn't been done before to maximize its reach and impact.

## Recommendations for Using Moden Technology to Advance Kawaida Philosophy

My recommendations include taking full advantage of every available opportunity to merge modern technology with the lessons of Kawaida for the win. Since victory in the struggle to create a good world is ultimately a numbers game, we must use every tool at our disposal to reach as many people as possible with the lessons of *"tradition and reason"* that Kawaida presents.

In turn, this becomes a direct way to build on the existing popularity of Kawaida through Kwanzaa and the Nguzo Saba / Seven Principles and to use these teachings directly to inspire more Black people to pursue careers and expertise in STEM disciplines – especially among young people. Surely, we need to apply that kind of foresight and planning, too, because it would certainly be wise to begin a program to create as many *sedjemic* STEM professionals as possible going forward as we search for those available now for our efforts today. This is also where efforts to advance the teachings would benefit greatly from an expansive children's program, a multifunction app, an online community, and from thoughtful engagement with and responses to the lingering controversies that challenge this goal.

There is also a critical need for us to begin using modern technology to develop our capacities for manufacturing. Beginning with basic household and novelty items is a great way to develop the STEM skillset needed to eventually begin producing items more critical to our survival.

In short, we are doing everything we recommend, and we encourage others to duplicate our efforts to whatever extent they can, or do something else completely different to assist in the effort to meet our people where they are to build on what they know. Because, indeed, if we know better, we will do better, and we should know that when we become the best version of ourselves in this way, people around the world will follow us and become the best possible version of themselves, too.

## C. Using Modern Technology to Advance Kawaida and Kawaida STEM to Realize Ourselves

I am convinced an effective merging of Kawaida with modern technology would lead to a range of improved outcomes for Black people and the broader society. If the tools, techniques, and potential of modern technology could be applied to increase understanding of the committed values-based focus of Kawaida, its focus on cultural development, and its expansive conception of Blackness, there is no doubt the world would be a better place. The vision for such an effort can be effectively described as a modern exercise in applying the Nguzo Saba / Seven Principles.

As things currently stand, Kawaida teachings through Kwanzaa and the Nguzo Saba / Seven Principles have an established presence on the internet and in other forms of modern technology. A variety of technical tools are also used to publish articles, interviews, and to host related efforts of Dr. Karenga and several long-time students of Kawaida who work diligently to share its teachings.

Yet there is considerable space, if not a considerable need, for additional and increased efforts at using the latest technical tools to expand the understanding and embrace of Kawaida, particularly the Nguzo Saba / Seven Principles and the Kawaida conception of Blackness.

While many different organizations and communities host their own Kwanzaa themed websites and related events, there is currently no central online location for people and organizations committed to these teachings to build together. Also, even though an app exists for seemingly every possible purpose these days, there are currently no apps that actively engage the teachings of Kawaida with the public as a daily vocation.

With these observations made by myself and other members of The Afrikan Restoration Project, we felt an obligation to use our knowledge and experience with modern technology to widely expand understanding and embrace of the Nguzo Saba / Seven Principles and the Kawaida conception of Blackness. In doing so, we set out to build on the work we started in 2017 when we began a major update to The Official Kwanzaa Website and created our own Kwanzaa themed website as a supplement.

At that time, we proposed a range of new ideas for using modern technology to advance the teachings. During the year 2023 we began doing our best work to complete most of them.

This resulted in a complete overhaul of our Kwanzaa website and the introduction of a brand-new website with a lot of modern bells and whistles at https://kwanzaa.org. This includes a new STEM based project titled "Nguzo Saba 365" that is designed to help make the Nguzo Saba / Seven Principles a daily vocation among Black people. With this program, we introduce a brand-new app for mobile phones that will allow us to use STEM to work actively with our members and partner organizations to promote the Seven Principles as a daily vocation and code of conduct.

Much of our work is on a new "Kwanzaa For Kids" program that uses online games, interactive media, and video instruction to advance our children's understanding of Kwanzaa and the Nguzo Saba with a focus on engaging and developing talents with STEM.

We focus on STEM throughout all our efforts and will offer a variety of STEM based activities and training for youth and adults. We also host our own instructional content instead of posting on platforms owned by others, and will make that same space available to create an online community practicing the values as a model to inspire more of the same.

As part of this program, we also resume our production of our original Kwanzaa and Nguzo Saba / Seven Principles themed products using some of the most modern production technology available. This work is part of a three-year initiative started in 2023 and leading up to the sixtieth anniversary of Kwanzaa in 2026 entitled "An Ujima Quest for a Kwanzaa Jubilee" – with three primary objectives.

The first objective is to merge the teachings Kawaida, Kwanzaa, and the Nguzo Saba / Seven Principles with modern technology in a way that has not been done before.

Our second objective is to expand understanding and embrace of the Nguzo Saba / Seven Principles, expand understanding of the Kwanzaa creation story, and to relentlessly promote the Kawaida conception of Blackness among Black people worldwide.

Our third objective is to clarify controversies linked to Kwanzaa from the COINTELPRO era by explaining our position on the substantive matters involved and why we made a range of conscious choices to not allow those concerns to prevent our understanding and embrace of some of our best teachings.

## D. Examples of Kawaida and Modern STEM Applied Now and Going Forward

The following images are screen captures from our new website and app that will be accessible through our https://kwanzaa.org website by the time this book is available. No images for our new and expanded section on the Nguzo Saba / Seven Principles or our expanded presentation of the Kwanza creation story are shown, as those are continuing to be developed when this book was delivered to the publisher. However, those entries will be accessible through our website and app by the time this book is available.

---

The New Kwanzaa.org Website Introduced in 2023
Sponsored by The Afrikan Restoration Project

The following images show the homepage of the new website we created in 2023 at https://kwanzaa.org. We will post a major update to this site by the start of Kwanzaa 2024, with continuing updates every year as we develop an online STEM based cultural community and promote our new app and initiative – Nguzo Saba 365.

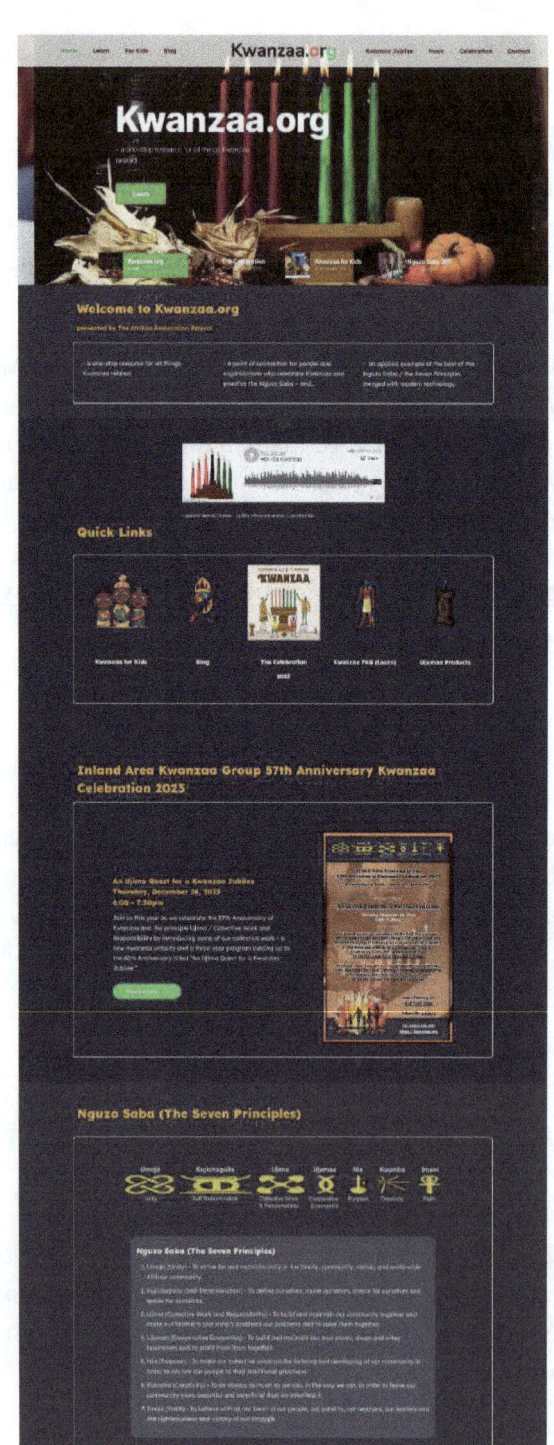

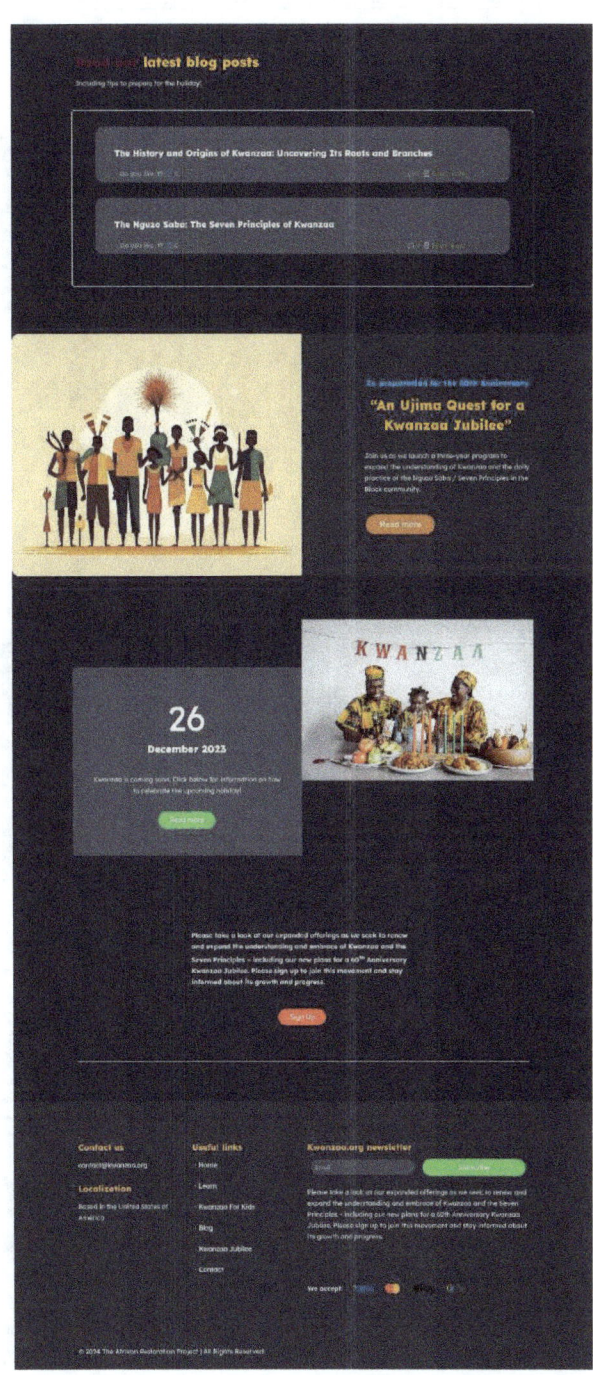

**latest blog posts**

Including tips to prepare for the holiday.

The History and Origins of Kwanzaa: Uncovering Its Roots and Branches

The Nguzo Saba: The Seven Principles of Kwanzaa

In preparation for the 60th Anniversary

**"An Ujima Quest for a Kwanzaa Jubilee"**

Join us as we launch a three-year program to expand the understanding of Kwanzaa and the daily practice of the Nguzo Saba / Seven Principles in the Black community.

Read more

**26**

December 2023

Kwanzaa is coming soon. Click below for information on how to celebrate the upcoming holiday!

Read more

Please take a look at our expanded offerings as we seek to renew and expand the understanding and embrace of Kwanzaa and the Seven Principles – including our new plans for a 60th Anniversary Kwanzaa Jubilee. Please sign up to join this movement and stay informed about its growth and progress.

Sign Up

**Contact us**

contact@kwanzaa.org

**Localization**

Based in the United States of America

**Useful links**

Home

Learn

Kwanzaa For Kids

Blog

Kwanzaa Jubilee

Connect

**Kwanzaa.org newsletter**

Subscribe

Please take a look at our expanded offerings as we seek to renew and expand the understanding and embrace of Kwanzaa and the Seven Principles – including our new plans for a 60th Anniversary Kwanzaa Jubilee. Please sign up to join this movement and stay informed about its growth and progress.

We accept:

© 2014 The African Restoration Project | All Rights Reserved

# – An Ujima Quest for a Kwanzaa Jubilee –
## *"Working to renew and increase understanding and embrace of Kwanzaa"*
https://kwanzaa.org/kwanzaa-jubilee

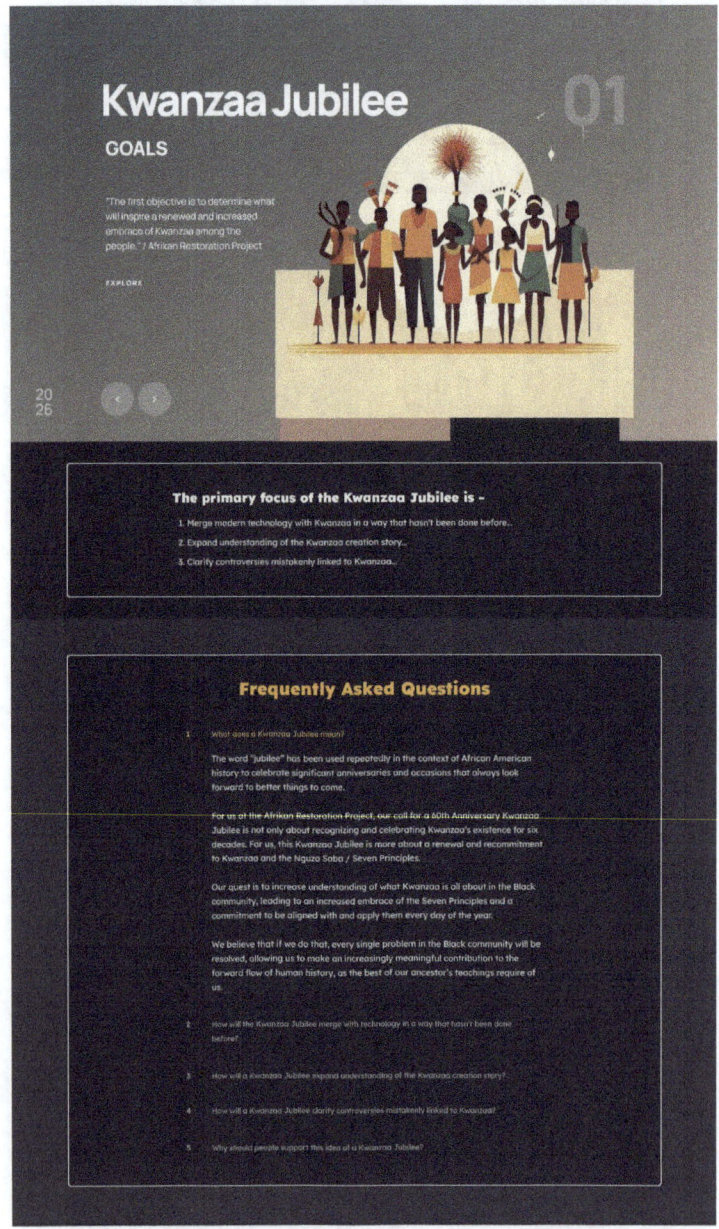

# – <u>Kwanzaa for Kids</u> –

*"Kwanzaa lessons, arts and crafts, download activities, storytelling, and more..."*

https://kwanzaa.org/kwanzaa-for-kids

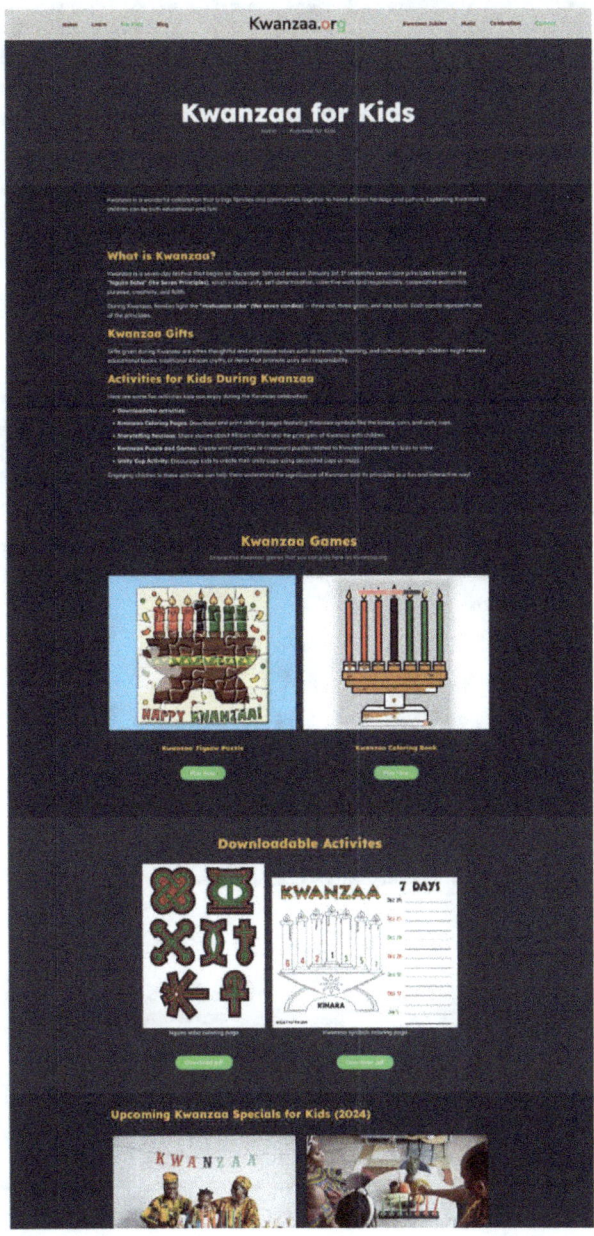

# – Kwanzaa for Kids –

*"Interactive games, arts and crafts video tutorials, STEM instruction, and more…"*

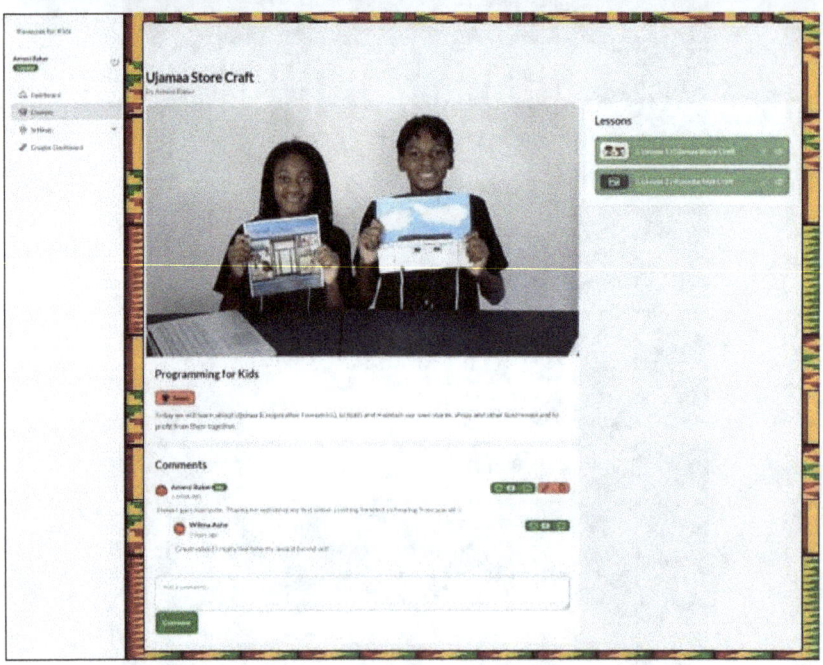

# – Nguzo Saba 365 Online Community –

*"Online space for members and partner organizations to post video content for STEM and cultural instruction"*

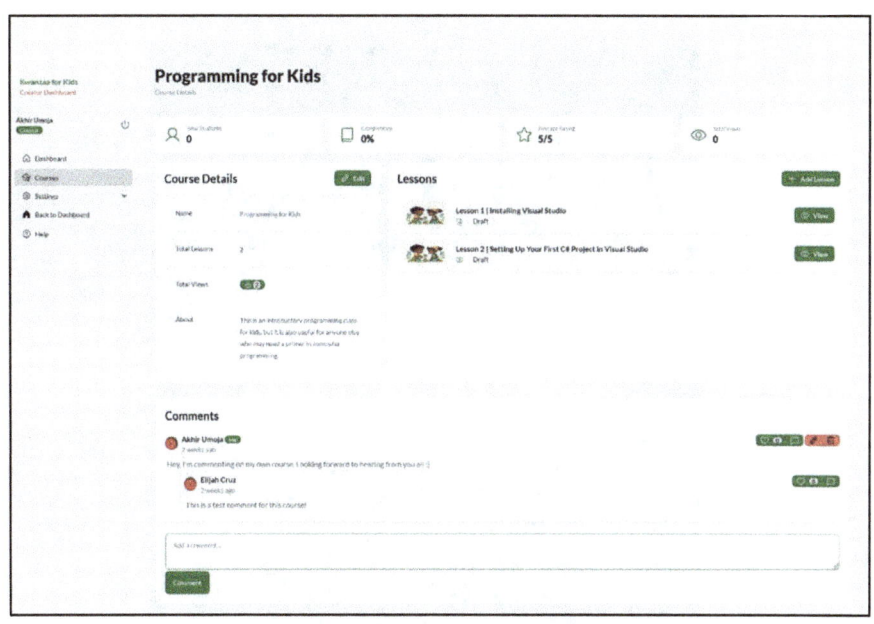

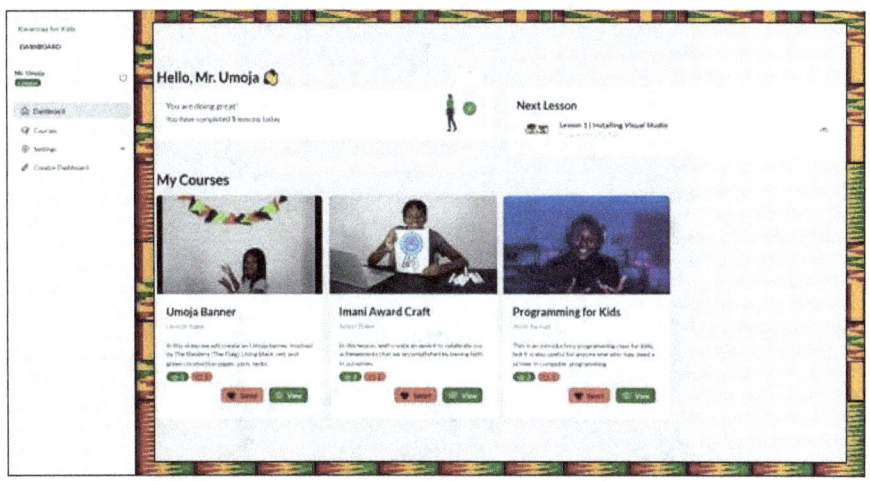

# – Kwanzaa.org Blog Sites –

*"Space for members and partner organizations to post written content for STEM and cultural instruction"*

https://kwanzaa.org/blog

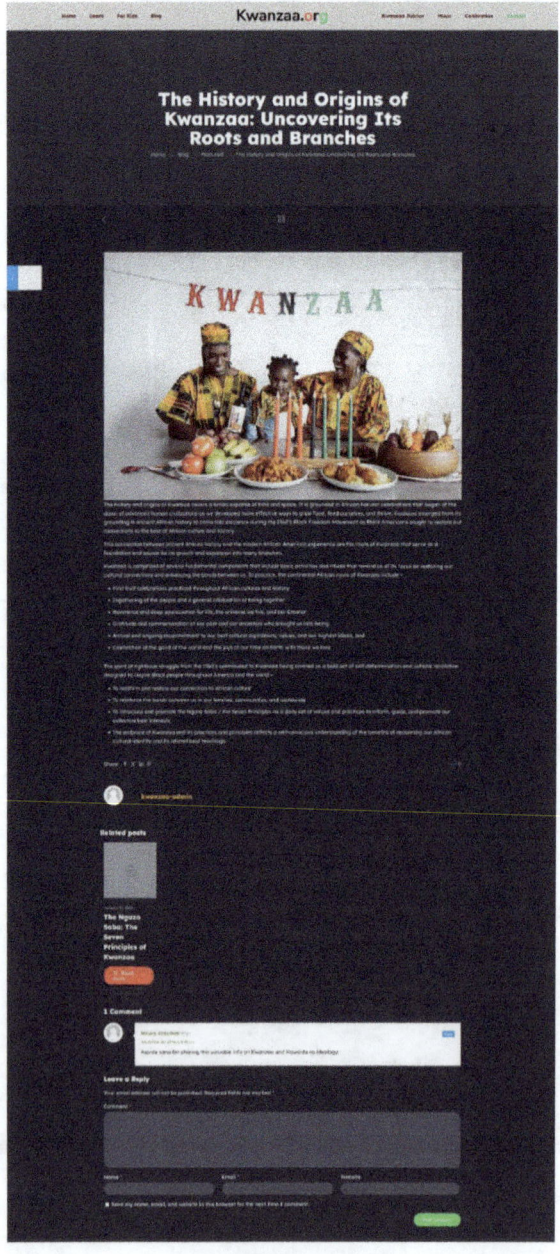

93

# An Ujimaa Quest for a Kwanzaa Jubilee | Part 1

Home — An Ujimaa Quest for a Kwanzaa Jubilee | Part 1

## An Ujima Quest for a Kwanzaa Jubilee: Using Tradition and Reason to Expand Our Understanding for Better Outcomes

Copyright © 2025 / Harold Shujaa Baker / All Rights Reserved

Whenever the word "Jubilee" is mentioned among Black people, a sacred event is soon coming. A big anniversary celebration, or a new phase of existence for us – or an honored tradition – is drawing near, and always with the hope and promise of better things to come.

Every Jubilee begins as a creative act of unity, purpose, and faith that becomes collective work and cooperative economics for people in route to self-determination. All Seven Principles apply on these occasions where we not only celebrate ourselves, but also renew our understanding of – and commitment to – those things that make us better people.

As the 57th season of Kwanzaa approaches and the 60th anniversary draws near, current circumstances give us reason to consider the need for a 60th Anniversary Kwanzaa Jubilee. That's because we are facing changes in this society of a level that hasn't occurred since the late 1960's, when Kwanzaa was first called for, created, and celebrated by the Us Organization (Us) – led by Dr. Maulana Karenga.

As part of our preparation and response, we need to infuse this year's Kwanzaa season with a spirit of renewal that brings forward an increased understanding and embrace of the holiday and the Seven Principles to help improve outcomes in all areas of Black life going forward.

To accomplish that, we need to bring more positive attention to the holiday than ever before to reach the critical majority who have not yet been reached and to reengage those who have or a higher level.

Although Kwanzaa is widely celebrated by Black people, most do not participate for various reasons. As Dr. Karenga has noted – "Kwanzaa is widespread, but not mainstream," Yet, at its best, it was conceived to have a positive, mainstream influence not yet fully achieved.

A primary reason for that is because the annual return of Kwanzaa prompts a return of the same anti- Kwanzaa attacks that happen every year, too. This contributes directly to the limited engagement with the holiday in the Black community.

Because of these things, many longtime Kwanzaa celebrants have hoped for and previously called for the type of renewal and recommitment represented by this call for a Kwanzaa Jubilee. But what does a Kwanzaa Jubilee mean in practice?

The first objective is to determine what will inspire a renewed and increased embrace of Kwanzaa among the people. Consistent with the communal spirit of the holiday, this jubilee would have to be a collective (Ujima) effort informed by teachings on Kwanzaa, the Nguzo Saba, and Kawaida philosophy – as developed by Dr. Karenga.

We reached out to request his participation from the start with no response so far. But we also understand the increasing demands on his time as Kwanzaa approaches. Ideally, this effort would gain his support, perhaps in an ever-increasing example of the shared good of Kwanzaa.

That's because no one can seriously claim to promote or represent Kwanzaa without respecting Dr. Karenga's contributions to it. Before Kwanzaa came into existence, he laid its foundation with his introduction of the Nguzo Saba (the Seven Principles) the year before (1965) and his development of the "cultural and social change philosophy" called Kawaida prior to that.

Kwanzaa became a way to introduce and link the Nguzo Saba with a Pan African tradition, while also advancing Kawaida. Dr. Karenga explains that – "Although the Nguzo Saba are most widely known as the Seven Principles of Kwanzaa, they are in a larger sense the Seven Principles of Kawaida philosophy, the cultural and social change philosophy out of which Kwanzaa and the Nguzo Saba were created."

So, after being inspired to create a Black holiday, Dr. Karenga organized and led the effort to create Kwanzaa. As a result, he is known worldwide as the holiday's sole creator, although he acknowledges others who assisted on occasion. He has also become a world class scholar, author, and professor of African history, culture, and ethics. His status as a leading scholar is well established.

But Kwanzaa emerged from a turbulent period in the late 1960's, and the Us Organization endured considerable losses. Despite Dr. Karenga's impressive achievements, negative stories from that era concerning him become the focus of the anti-Kwanzaa attacks we face each year. As the sole creator of Kwanzaa, criticism of him is directly linked to the holiday, causing many to dismiss his work. But the ideas behind Kwanzaa are much bigger than any one person or their shortcomings - real or imagined - even the holiday's creator, and I think he would agree.

So, how do we advance the shared good and ethical focus of Kwanzaa beyond these concerns?

Clarifying negative stories about Dr. Karenga is a necessary step, particularly, where distinguishing those matters from Kwanzaa is concerned. Some of the biggest issues can be easily resolved by studying verified sources. The most controversial topics are still affected by negative internal and external influences that prevent the highest possible lessons and insight from emerging. We will address this in more detail going forward.

For now, a creative focus directly contributing to a Kwanzaa renewal or jubilee would be to expand our understanding of the Kwanzaa creation story by considering the people who inspired and assisted Dr. Karenga in the process. A range of new and inspiring conversations could be created about the people involved in an effort aligned with the communal nature of Kwanzaa and the Seven Principles.

Being known as the sole creator of Kwanzaa has elevated Dr. Karenga's global status, but it is also departs from

94

# – The "Nguzo Saba 365" App –

*"A multi-function app to help us practice the Nguzo Saba every day of the year"*

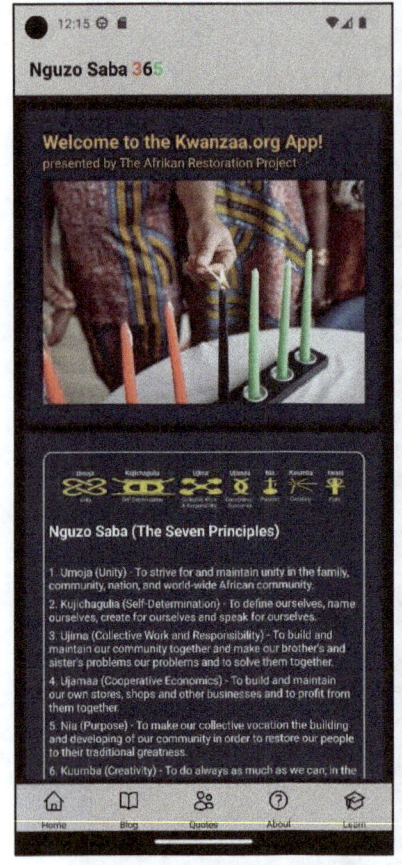

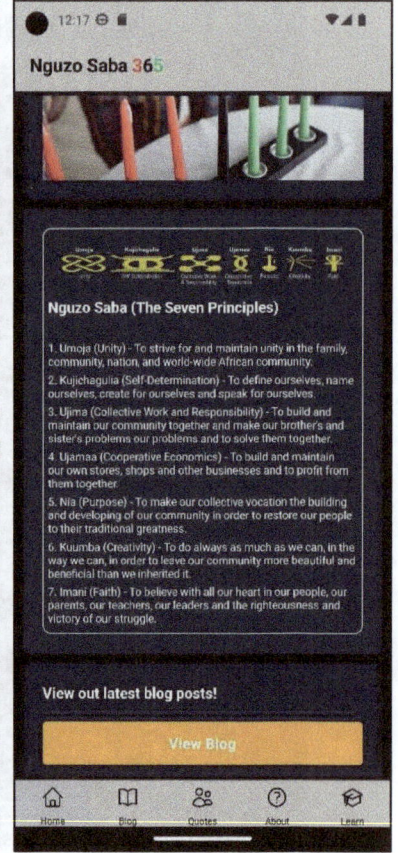

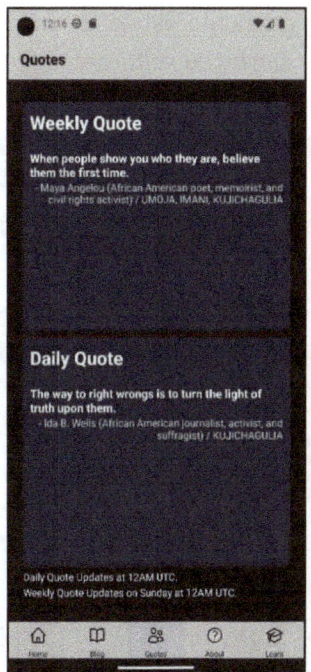

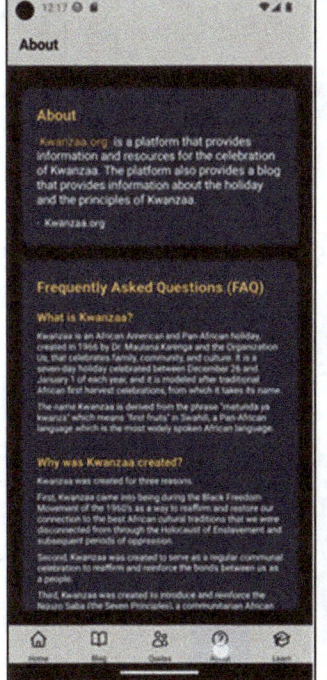

# – <u>Kwanzaa.shop / Ujamaa Marketplace</u> –
### *"Online store featuring custom designed cultural products we manufacture ourselves"*

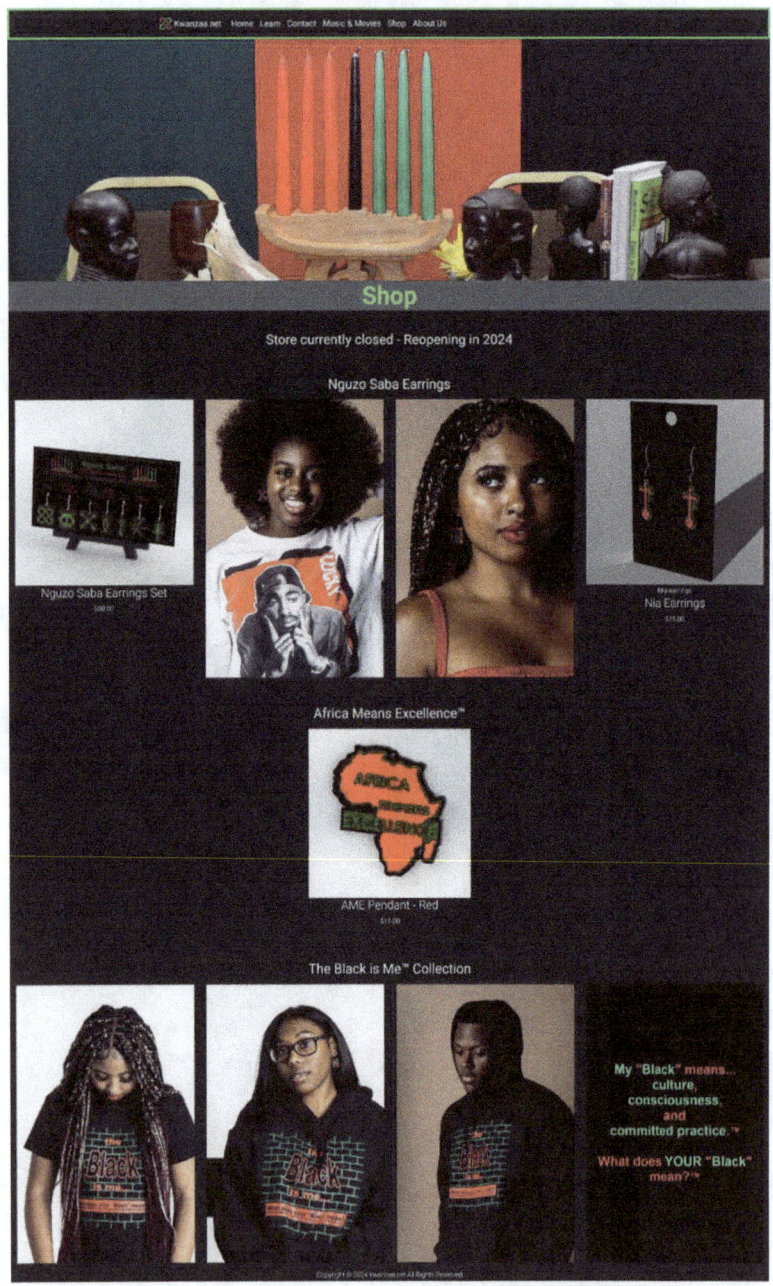

## FEATURED PRODUCTS

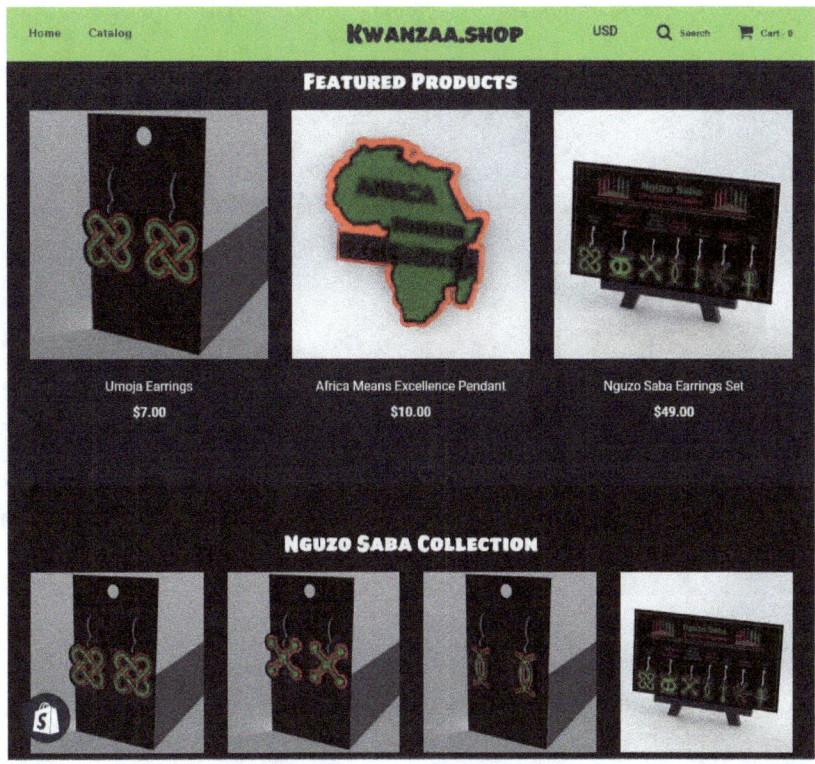

Umoja Earrings
$7.00

Africa Means Excellence Pendant
$10.00

Nguzo Saba Earrings Set
$49.00

## NGUZO SABA COLLECTION

98

## AFRICA MEANS EXCELLENCE COLLECTION

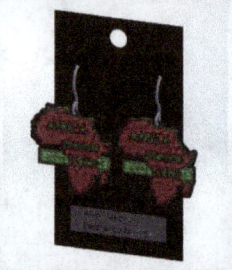

Africa Means Excellence Magnent
$10.00

Africa Means Excellence Earrings (Red)
$12.00

Africa Means Excellence Pendant
$10.00

## NGUZO SABA NECKLACES

Nguzo Saba Imani Necklace
$10.00

Nguzo Saba Kuumba Necklace
$10.00

Nguzo Saba Nia Necklace
$10.00

Nguzo Saba Ujamaa Necklace
$10.00

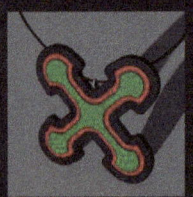

Nguzo Saba Ujima Necklace
$10.00

Nguzo Saba Kujichagulia
Necklace
$10.00

Nguzo Saba Umoja Necklace
$10.00

## E.  Highest Short-Term Aspirations for Kawaida STEM

Our highest aspirations in the short term certainly include a successful launch of our new website, app, and online community. But there are two other projects that fall in this category, each with its own significant meaning and STEM focus consistent with Kawaida teachings presented here.

In the section where we discussed the benefits of mastering ancient, modern, and future technology, we introduced the idea of contributing to the design of a scaled model of the Great Pyramid of Giza where we would demonstrate the ancient technology still in place there today confirming it was built to function as an ancient electrical power plant.

Discoveries noted in the book titled "The Giza Power Plant: Technologies of Ancient Egypt" [18, 19] by longtime engineer, Christopher Dunn, and other sources can inform this work. With a qualified team of scientists, physicists, and engineers this goal could be accomplished in the short term. This would not only confirm another significant contribution and benefit the modern world gained from ancient Kemet, but it would also pose prospects for environmentally responsible energy production today, as a Kawaida STEM focus requires.

I'm ready to apply my skills to help get it done. Who will join me?

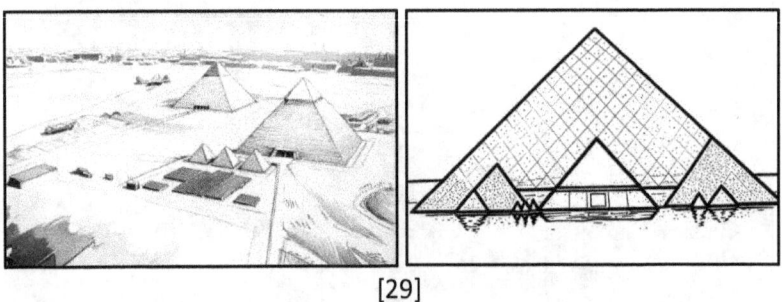

[29]

Finally, completing the second project on the list of our highest short-term aspirations would require us to practice every one of the Seven Principles at the highest level. The design and construction of a new,

101

multi-level, multi-function facility based on ancient and contemporary African architectural styles with modern amenities would require every principle be applied – Umoja/Unity, Kujichagulia/Self Determination, Ujima/Collective Work, Ujamaa/Cooperative Economics, Nia/Purpose, Kuumba/Creativity, and Imani/Faith – to be achieved.

This new facility, first conceived decades ago, would become "The International Kwanzaa Headquarters."

Architectural renderings were created years ago after the idea was introduced, but there has been no effort to complete the project in recent years. When I heard about it almost two decades ago, I thought it was a great idea that needed the benefit of modern technology to make it happen. We now have a well-developed, STEM based proposal to complete the project.

The images below show a 3D concept model of a four-story, multi-function facility we created, equipped with an African cultural flair and the most modern amenities. We continue to look forward to the prospect of this long-held vision being realized and we are eager to lend our design, animation, coding, and STEM based talents overall for its completion.

## F. Conclusion: Forward Trajectories for Kawaida STEM and the Kawaida Conception of Blackness

From where I stand, the future for Kawaida STEM looks bright. We have invested our best efforts to build on the work done by Dr. Karenga and the elders, ancestors, and contemporary scholars who inspired his work. We hope and believe our best efforts to remind the Black community of our expansive, world leading history as innovators of STEM will be well received by the people.

I also hope an increasing number of our people will embrace the Kawaida conception of Blackness as they learn about its depth as a cultural idea. The *"unbudging Blackness"* of Kawaida offers great benefit for all who embrace its elevated ideas as compared to diminished ideas and stereotypes about Blackness in race propaganda. An elevated self-conception is the first required step towards doing truly elevated things, and is a necessary step for us to transform all negative circumstances affecting us into positive outcomes.

Yet, like everything else in existence, Kawaida STEM and Kawaida philosophy more broadly are subject to the same sudden or slow fade into non-existence if they don't evolve in the most thoughtful and spirited way possible. We certainly hope our work contributes to these teachings lasting for eternity, or for as long as the human family exists on Earth.

If our objectives are met, more and more Black people will prepare themselves to master every STEM discipline and profession in existence, while bringing communal African values and a commitment to stand worthy before other people, the natural world, and the divine forces that make our existence possible in the process.

We will only be successful in this work if we achieve these outcomes, and if our elders and ancestors are satisfied with our efforts.

In closing, I say asante sana sana (Thank you very much) to Dr. Karenga for the inspiration of his life's work and to all the other elders and ancestors who inspire all of us to do as Franz Fanon advised when he called on all of us to *"...discover [our] mission and either fulfill it or betray it..."* – as we try to fulfill ours...

## References

1) Kawaida Theory: An Introductory Outline / 1980, Maulana Karenga

2) Selections from The Husia: Sacred Wisdom of Ancient Egypt / 1984, Maulana Karenga

3) The Book of Coming Forth by Day / 1990, Maulana Karenga

4) The Million Man March Day of Absence Mission Statement / 1996, Maulana Karenga

5) Odù Ifá: The Ethical Teachings – A Kawaida Interpretation / 1999, Maulana Karenga

6) Maat: The Moral Ideal in Ancient Egypt / 2004, Maulana Karenga

7) Kawaida and Questions of Life and Struggle / 2008, Maulana Karenga

8) Kwanzaa: A Celebration of Family, Community, and Culture / 2008 (1998), Maulana Karenga

9) Introduction to Black Studies (Fourth Edition) / 2010, Maulana Karenga

10) The Message and Meaning of Kwanzaa: Bringing Good into the World / 2016, M. Karenga

11) Repairing and Remaking the World: An Environmental Vision of Justice / 2017, M. Karenga

12) Retrieving the African Ideal: A Courageous Questioning in These Times / 2018, M. Karenga

13) Earth, Wind, Water and Fire: Saving Ourselves and the World / 2019, Maulana Karenga

14) The Autobiography of Malcolm X (As Told to Alex Haley) / 1964, Malcolm X and Alex Haley

15) Malcolm X: Speeches at Harvard / 1991, Archie Epps

16) Personal notes from varied lectures by Dr. Karenga

17) Dr. Fauci Warned In 2017 Of 'Surprise Outbreak' During Trump Administration – [https://www.huffpost.com/entry/fauci-warned-of-trump-pandemic-2017_n_5e8a0548c5b6e7d76c65c8a4]

18) The Giza Power Plant: Technologies of Ancient Egypt / 1998, Christopher Dunn

19) Afrikan Restoration Project / Pomona – Book review for "The Giza Power Plant: Technologies of Ancient Egypt" by Christopher Dunn, presented by Shujaa Baker
https://youtu.be/I9aE5B31wr4?si=8sWfnsFBH6zrR2gF

20) The Ankh: African Origin of Electromagnetism / 1997, Nur Ankh Amen

21) SAMPIE (Solar Array Module Plasma Interaction Experiment) –
https://www.youtube.com/watch?v=5Nh3yAAw_Ko

22) Microscale Hydrodynamics Near Moving Contact Lines –
https://ntrs.nasa.gov/citations/19950008122

23) Guion Bluford Bio -
https://www.nasa.gov/sites/default/files/atoms/files/bluford_guion.pdf

24) Earl 5X Grant Memorial Program / June 2019, Tehuti Kambui

25) Audio Recording, Conversation with Earl 5X Grant / July 2015, Shujaa Baker

26) Farewell to Another Pan-African Warrior / 2019, A. Peter Bailey –
https://flcourier.com/farewell-to-another-pan-african-warrior/

27) <u>The Art of War</u> / Sun Tzu / Teachings on Tao (compelling unity through moral law)

28) <u>SD's Black Panther Party Celebrates 55<sup>th</sup> Anniversary with Peace Treaty</u> / <u>https://sdnews.com/sds-black-panther-party-celebrates-55th-anniversary-with-peace-treaty</u>

29) Images from a soon to be released book on African / Kemetic architecture titled "<u>Kmt Architecture Revisited</u>" by Dr. Tdka Maat Kilimanjaro

30) <u>Birth of a White Nation: The Invention of White People and its Relevance Today</u> / 2013 , Jacqueline Battalora

www.ingramcontent.com/pod-product-compliance
Lightning Source LLC
Chambersburg PA
CBHW070758120626
46557CB00002B/660